KILLING RAGE

Less than two weeks after June Stotts' mutilated body was discovered, Arthur Shawcross picked up his next victim, prostitute Darlene Trippi. They drove to a deserted truck lot and parked behind three abandoned tractor trailers.

He gave her thirty dollars but soon realized she could not satisfy him. Shawcross called her no good and demanded his money back. Trippi made fun of his manhood, and when he tried to take his money back, she fought him.

It was the last thing she would ever do.

Striking out in blind anger, Shawcross pushed hard against her chin, pinning her to the car door. He kept on pressing, choking off her air as the chin dug deeper and deeper into her windpipe. Finally she stopped kicking and struggling and went limp.

Sweat pouring off him onto the naked corpse, Shawcross sat there quietly for hours, waiting for the strange calm to come over him again. Soon the identity of Darlene Trippi would fade into the blur of women he'd killed and he could go home to dinner.

ARTHUR SHAWCROSS: THE GENESEE RIVER KILLER

The Grisly True Crime Account
of the
Rochester Prostitute Murders!

DR. JOEL NORRIS

PINNACLE BOOKS
WINDSOR PUBLISHING CORP.

*DEDICATED TO MY STEADFAST SUP-
PORTERS Marguriete Jones McKinney and to the
Memory of Melvin David Maurer.*

PINNACLE BOOKS

are published by

Windsor Publishing Corp.
475 Park Avenue South
New York, NY 10016

Copyright © 1992 by Dr. Joel Norris
and Shadow Lawn Press

First printing: January, 1992

Printed in the United States of America

ACKNOWLEDGMENTS

Paul Dinas, Editor at Zebra, for his understanding of the importance of this research; Ronald C. and Heather Valentine, Shawcross' attorney and his wife, for their lifetime work in understanding criminal behavior; David Murante, Rochester Defense Attorney; Charles Siragusa, Rochester Prosecuting Attorney; Dr. Park Dietz; Dr. Vernon Mark, Neurologist Professor Emeritus, Harvard; Dr. William Walsh, Biochemist, Chicago, Illinois; Dr. John Money, Forensic Sexologist, Baltimore, Maryland; Dr. Richard Kraus, Wayne County Psychiatrist for the defense; Investigators Bruce Lisenio, Ray Herald; and, New York secretaries Phyllis Bleik and Linda Stutton. And, to my personal assistants and friends, Judy Lawrence Mahoney, Linda Sheppard Storey, and Ute Musselman, who in the process of assisting me learned more about serial killers than anyone wants to know.

Introduction

In June, 1990, I received a call in San Francisco from Ronald C. Valentine, the Public Defender of Wayne County, New York. He had read my book *Serial Killers—A Growing Menace,* and was defending a 44-year-old white male, Arthur J. Shawcross, who had confessed to serially killing eleven female prostitutes and/or street women in Rochester, New York over the past year.

His client closely fit the profile of a serial killer featured in the book. For the past fifteen years, I have researched the cause of serial murder. Each new case verified the original profile and also opened new areas to be researched.

There were to be two trials in upstate New York; one in Rochester, Monroe County, for ten of the killings, and a second trial in adjoining Wayne County where the body of one of the women killed was dumped. David Murante, the Rochester lawyer, and Mr. Valentine were mounting an insanity defense and were sharing experts. Their mutual communities were committed to funding an extensive evaluation of Mr.

Shawcross and his state of mind. Arthur Shawcross was about to become one of the most thoroughly researched serial killers of our time.

The death penalty was not a direct issue in the case, because New York State has no death penalty, but precedents needed to be set in New York to assure that exploratory diagnosis (i.e., biochemical, neurological, and neuropsychological testing) be made available to those accused of violent behavior to assure that they had received the best available diagnosis for their defense.

I had heard about the case through the media and in conversations with law enforcement officials who were working on other prostitute cases in other parts of the country. I know about serial killer prostitute cases in Alabama; Florida; Boston and New Bedford, Massachusetts; San Diego and Los Angeles, California; and, of course Seattle, Washington, where the undiscovered Green River Killer has become infamous. I knew that prostitutes, both male and female, are a prime target group for serial killers because of their availability as potential victims and the variety of symbolic projections placed upon them by society. I knew such a visible, available, and vulnerable symbol could become a target for years of built up hatred of women in general, and I knew that a deep love/hate relationship with an abusive or neglectful mother or ex-wife was involved. I also understood how the tragic victims had become puppets receiving the rage of the killer's severely brutally violent sexual fantasies. I also knew that such behavior did not occur in a vacuum. There were multiple and complex causes.

There was some immediacy in pulling the case together for a September trial. It wouldn't be possible for me to travel to New York until after the Fourth of July, but I agreed to have Ron send me some of the case material. A few days later, a box full of printed material arrived — confessions; mental health, prison, arrest, medical, and parole records; newspaper clippings; and, a journal written by Arthur Shawcross himself.

Immediately, familiar patterns began to emerge and for the next several months I worked almost exclusively on this case.

In July, I finally met Arthur Shawcross. My first impression was that he appeared older than his 44 years, even though overweight he was robust, and had very large massive forearms and very strong mit-like hands. I interviewed him for at least 24 hours in 5 different sessions. He had already been interviewed by numerous psychologists, psychiatrists, law enforcement officials, etc., yet he persevered in telling his story one more time. I observed three emotional states exhibited by Mr. Shawcross. During most of the interviews, his affect was flat with little or no emotion. It would change, however, to a deep genuine sadness when he mentioned his mother, and to a quick genuinely angry outburst of emotion when he was not understood. His verbalization was tedious and excessive in that it took him a long time to get to the point he was trying to make. Like other serial killers with excessive verbosity, he showed feeble attempts at humor that were indeed not humorous. This behavior is a soft sign of possible brain damage. Even though verbally his affect was flat and there was no showing of remorse when he spoke about the crimes, his large hands, which were his

9

weapons, were very active during different phases of questioning. He would clasp his hands together or wring them as if they were activating all of the emotions of this brute of a man. When he would hold up his hands to demonstrate how he killed his victims, one could easily see how these women were helpless at their moment of death. Always present at the interviews was Ron Valentine; Ron's investigator, Bruce Lisenio; and/or David Murante. All interviews were videotaped.

The interviews were conducted on the third floor of the Monroe County jail, comfortably air conditioned to house the hundreds of people—inmates and workers—that inhabit its space on a daily basis. Mr. Shawcross was consistently cooperative, even allowing his hair to be clipped to the skull when samples were being sent for biochemical analysis to Illinois. The interviews were congenial and Mr. Shawcross seemed eager to please all around him, and easily was the epitome of an upstate New York good old boy.

After leaving Rochester, I took the next couple of months consulting with some of the leading experts in the country from the fields of neurology, psychiatry, psychology, biology, sexology, criminal justice, and post traumatic stress disturbance. We also conducted the most extensive computer search ever done looking for professional articles written in the last ten years from the above mentioned fields concerning the variety of probable causes of Mr. Shawcross' violent behavior. We discovered over 50,000 citations.

I believe that this is the most researched case concerning the roots of serial violence ever performed. The most alarming discovery of all was the reaffirmation that, like most serial murder cases I know about, these murders could have been prevented. The findings of the study and the demonstration of several missed opportunities for intervention are what this book is about.

Dr. Joel Norris
October, 1991

Chapter 1
Little Man

Arthur Shawcross liked driving Clara Neal's car. It was rented, and she let him take it wherever he wanted. It was still relatively new, and Artie hadn't driven much since he'd gotten out of prison. He didn't even have a license. He liked the car's color, too, a nice light blue-gray. He hadn't seen cars this color when they'd sent him up for murder fifteen years earlier. His wife, Rose Marie Walley, knew that Clara Neal was Art's friend. But Art told her he was being nice to her just so he could drive her car. Rose didn't make an issue of it. "A man's got to have friends," she told Rochester police investigator Mark Kelley after Art was arrested. She just let her Artie go off whenever he wanted, never challenging him about where he was going or who he was seeing. And in return Artie was kind. He was understanding. He gave her companionship. She said she loved him no matter what he did. Arthur Shawcross was driving that Omni on the nights he committed some of his prostitute murders.

Rose told the police that she noticed one of the first real changes in Arthur Shawcross when his parents didn't show up for Christmas in 1987. They went to visit his sister, Jeannie instead. In January, Arthur had said, he asked his parents to come for a visit. But they never came. Instead, they returned the "Jesus" clock that Arthur had ordered from a Fingerhut catalog. He said that he had saved up the money he'd earned in prison, about $60, for the gift and had had it sent to his mother mail order. "It had a picture of the Lord onto it," Rose told the police. His mother had told his sister Jeannie in Virginia when she'd visited her over Christmas that it was "trashy."

Arthur walked into the bathroom and slammed the door behind him when he heard the news about his parents' going to Virginia, and he beat on the walls until he started crying. Then he got on his bicycle and rode until he felt better. Rose told the police that the coldness of his mother settled over the household like the January chill that had settled over all of Rochester in 1988. He didn't want to be in Rochester because he felt isolated. He wanted to be near Rose's family. But the parole board settled him in Rochester and had him working out of the labor pool at Clinton North ever since the New York State probation department had moved him there from the rural town of Vestal, New York, just outside Binghamton.

They couldn't stay in the Binghamton area, nor in Delhi, nor in Fleischmanns, nor anywhere else where people had learned that he was a convicted child murderer who had also raped and sodomized a little girl and buried her alive in soft dirt until she suffocated, though he was never charged for those crimes. That was one of the reasons he was out on parole after serving only fifteen years. He had been raped himself

14

when he was in prison. Inmates don't like "short eyes."

His parole didn't sit well with the Binghamton police department or with the mayor of Fleischmanns, who led a delegation of citizens to his apartment building in the middle of the night and, by the light of burning torches, attempted to drive him out of town. His parole officer and the deputy sheriff had arrived just before violence broke out to spirit Arthur Shawcross and his girlfriend Rose Marie Walley out of town. They placed the family in Rochester, where they were moved into a studio apartment on Alexander Street. At first he was working out of the Kelly Temporary Services labor pool, where he would report early each morning for placement and would receive about $3.75 an hour. Then he got a job preparing vegetables at Brognia Brothers Produce, where he was working when his mother refused to visit him over Christmas.

Shawcross never told owner Fred Brognia that he was on parole for murdering children. At first he told him that he'd killed a drunken driver who'd killed his wife and son. Another time he told Brognia that he'd been a "hitter" for organized-crime families in New York City.

Arthur tried to tell Rose how much it hurt him that his mother wouldn't talk to him. They hadn't spoken in over fifteen years, but she had remained close to his sister, which also hurt Art, Rose said. Almost a year later Shawcross himself would tell a California psychiatrist working for Monroe County prosecutor Chuck Siragusa that when he was a young boy his sister was one of the first people to introduce him to sex and allowed him to sodomize her. His sister has consistently denied these statements.

Shawcross continued for the rest of the month to be sullen and bitter about his mother's not visiting him over Christmas or in January 1988. Whenever he was feeling mad, Rose said, he would get on his bike and disappear until he felt better. That was why she thought nothing of it when, at about seven on a very cold Friday evening in February 1988, with a light layer of frozen snow on the ground, Artie said he had to go out on his bike again. He didn't tell her that the "sweats" were upon him or that he felt weird, as if there was a translucent envelope separating him from the rest of the world. He didn't tell her this time that he was getting one of his "headaches," the ones that made him almost blind with pain, sick to his stomach, and feeling the panic he'd felt when he was in Vietnam, he'd once told her, with the droning helicopters filling the air everywhere with their throbbing and their rotors beating down the tall bamboo grass with their propwash.

Why was he sweating so hard, Shawcross asked himself as he got on his bike and began riding. There was a hard layer of snow on the ground. It was an upper New York State winter deep freeze, yet he was sweating right through his shirt. He went over to Clara's and picked up her Dodge and went driving. He just had to drive, put miles on the car, troll along the backroads and state routes as if he were out fishing or hunting during the day. He liked fishing, Rose told the police after Artie's arrest. And he liked hunting, too. He liked anything where he could be alone for long periods of time, trolling along the water's edge or cruising through the woods. He would go off on his bike, pick up Clara's car, and take it fishing and hunting. then he

16

would come back. He once told Rose that as soon as he got his own license, he'd get his own car and break things off with Clara Neal. "It wasn't even romantic," Rose told the police.

Arthur Shawcross also said he liked to be alone. Sometimes it was like when he was in Vietnam, he once told psychiatrists, where he'd drive from firebase to firebase all by himself, hauling ammo to the remote hilltop redouts where the grunts would keep watch on the Vietcong infiltration routes into the Central Highlands. He was his own man in Vietnam, he told psychiatrists. Even the VC were afraid of him, he bragged, because of what he did to their women.

That night in February, as Rose Walley Shawcross saw Arthur ride away and disappear into the February night, she didn't now where he was going. In fact, Artie had taken his bike to see his girlfriend Clara Neal. He spent the evening with her, he said, and then kept her car overnight. But instead of taking it back home to Alexander Street, he went driving through a familiar industrial area of Rochester notorious for being the red-light district on Lake Avenue near the Genesee River. Arthur had been there before, cruising the streets in this section of town which had become a haven for the homeless and the drug pushers, $25-a-night prostitutes, and runaways from the rural towns in the northern part of the state.

"Dotsie" Blackburn thought she recognized the blue Dodge as she stepped out into the street. She thought she'd seen the driver before, but it was dark and she couldn't be sure. Maybe this was the guy some of the other girls called Mitch. She walked right in front of the car, Shawcross told police, and when he stopped, she opened the door and got in.

"Want a date?" she asked.

"Okay," Shawcross remembers telling her. "Where do we go?"

"Drive," Dorothy Blackburn said, and began directing Shawcross down Lake Avenue, past Lyell Avenue, toward West Main Street. Big warehouses in that section of town loomed out of the early evening darkness.

"Down there?" Shawcross asked, pointing to Nick Trahou's restaurant off in the distance.

"Dummy!" Blackburn said as she laughed. "Go around behind it, in the parking lot." Maybe he was only kidding her, she might have thought.

They pulled into an industrial parking lot behind a warehouse and Artie put the transmission in park while he left the engine running and the heater on. Sweat was pouring off him, but he didn't know if the girl was cold. After all, she'd been walking around in the subfreezing air since dark, probably.

"Wanna fuck?" Dotsie asked him as she turned to face him.

"How much?" Shawcross asked.

"You want a blow job or a half blow job—half screw?" she asked back.

"How much?"

"I get $20 for a blow job, $30 for a half-and-half," she said.

Shawcross took $30 out of his wallet and handed it over.

"I want to eat you while you give me a blow job," he said.

Dotsie Blackburn didn't answer. The car was already getting too warm for her and the windows were beginning to steam. She took off her pants, under-wear, shoes, and hose and shifted around under him. Artie unzipped his fly, he told the police almost a year later, shifted around until he was on top of Dotsie, and dropped his penis into her mouth. Nothing happened.

"Maybe we were doing it for three or so minutes," Shawcross told police. "And it felt good." But he still couldn't get an erection. No matter. Arthur said that he kept on pumping and pressing into her with his tongue, oblivious to anything else. Then, suddenly, he felt a searing, burning pain in his penis that wouldn't stop.

She was biting into his dick, he realized as he wrenched in agony and convulsively tried to jerk his penis from between her clenched teeth. He screamed and looked down. His skin was torn open and there was blood spurting out all over the front seat of the car. At the very first, Shawcross told investigators, he thought he was going to die because there was so much blood. He grabbed his penis and screamed at her. Then he looked into her smiling, bloody face. The whore was grinning through his own blood, he realized. He swooped down and bit into her vagina as hard as he could and pulled back with his teeth.

"Something tore loose," he told investigators a year later.

Then he looked down and saw that she was also bleeding. But she was also still smiling at his holding on to his penis to try to stop the blood flow. Shawcross said that with his right hand he squeezed her throat until she lost consciousness. Then he got out of the car, took some Handi Wipes out of the glove compartment, and wrapped them around his penis to absorb the blood. Then he zipped his fly and climbed back into the car. Dorothy Blackburn was still unconscious but breathing easily. He sat her up, put her head back against the seat, and tied her arms behind her with her pants.

Blackburn came to and struggled against the bonds.

"What are you doing?" she mumbled.

"Shut up," he barked back at her.

He looked around to make sure that they were still alone. It was still early and he could hear the noise from the restaurant, but there was no one in the parking lot. The warehouses were closed.

He gave Blackburn a coldly menacing look. She was still trying to pull her hands out of the knots and seemed not to realize that she was in a dangerous situation.

"I'm not the same person you got into the car with," he said, but she gave him no reaction. Shawcross started the car, dropped it into gear, and rolled it toward the entrance of the parking lot, but then turned around to face her. She stared directly into his eyes and didn't even blink. He could tell that even in the dark. Her look was demeaning, defiant. He grabbed her by the hair as hard as he could, yanking it up by its roots until he felt the scalp give, and snapped her head back against the front seat.

"Why'd you bite me?" he demanded.

She didn't answer. He pulled harder.

"Because I felt like it," she hissed.

Shawcross took Dorothy Blackburn's shirt and tied her feet together so she couldn't kick and couldn't get in the way of his driving. Then he headed out of the parking lot and drove west along State Route 104 until

20

he came to Northampton Park. He pulled over by a small bridge over Salmon Creek where, his wife Rose later told police, he liked to fish whenever he had to be alone. He'd go there after talking with his mother on the phone or after a hard day at the food processing plant. "He could cook salmon hundreds of ways," Rose had said when they'd interviewed her after Art's arrest.

There was a small chain across the road leading to the bridge, Art remembered, and he stopped the car there rather than take the chain down. Then he turned to face Blackburn again. She was still glaring at him with a defiance that only drove him into a deeper fury. He cocked his hand and slapped her across her face with all his might. She yelped, but didn't sob or cry. She just stared. Then he took the flashlight that he carried in the glove compartment and stared at his penis, which was now bleeding through the Handi Wipes. He remembered that it was "a bloody mess."

"Why'd you bite me?" he asked again.

" 'Cause I felt like it," she said, this time with something like a note of triumph in her voice.

"I won't be able to love a woman again," Shawcross told police he moaned as he inspected the torn and bleeding skin on his penis. He said he told her that she had ruined him, but that she only laughed. "She started calling me 'little man,' 'faggot' and 'queer,' " he said to the investigators. "Then she started cursing me."

Shawcross took off his pants and stepped out onto the cold, snowy ground, where he packed his penis with the icy snow that was still clean. At first the cold seared him worse than the burning sensation from the

21

bleeding wound, but it eventually took the pain away and the bleeding slowly stopped. Then Shawcross packed more ice and snow around new Handi Wipes and pulled a condom over his penis to keep his make-shift bandage and dressing in place. He was in intense pain, he remembered, and had to do it slowly while Dotsie watched him from inside the car. Then he climbed back into the front seat and stared at her again. She kept on watching him as if she were looking at an animal.

"I'm gonna rape you," he hissed at her.

Dotsie laughed into Artie's face, her bloodstained lips making a gruesome sight in the darkness. Shawcross began to sweat even worse, steaming up the windows with his body heat, and yanked her across the front seat. He pulled her as close to him as he could and began fondling her breasts. She didn't fight him but became limp; it was as if he were handling a fish on the deck of a boat. He chewed on her ear, getting no response, and then whispered, "You're gonna die. What do you have to say about that?"

She only smiled at him, and he thought as he looked at her bloody lips, he would say a year later, that she might have been on drugs. He slowly untied her feet and hands, keeping his hands on her all the time to let her know that he could have killed her at any moment, and then told her to get dressed.

Maybe Dorothy Blackburn thought Shawcross was going to let her go. Maybe she thought that she had stood up to him and won. But whatever she was think-ing, she spat out, "little man," and started laughing again.

In an instant Shawcross seized her throat, snapping

22

her head back with the breadth of his handspan, and locked his elbows as he crushed her neck in his fingers. His hands were powerful from ripping apart the flesh from the game he'd butcher after hunting, and he could feel her neck collapse under his grip. He was almost in a convulsive spasm from the fury that was overwhelming him at the same time, squeezing and crushing, shaking and pressing for "a good ten minutes," he told investigators.

At first Dorothy Blackburn went rigid, her back arching from the pain and the panic at suffocation. Then, after a few minutes, Shawcross remembered, she went limp against the seat as he kept on choking her. He released her and let her slump back onto the seat and against the door.

Arthur Shawcross remembered that he slowly began to calm down after he let her go. She could have even been asleep if it weren't for the fact that she wasn't breathing. He just stared at her as he let the backwash of his fury pass through him. His own breathing slowed and he began to feel chilly. He had sweated right through all the clothing he was wearing and was now beginning to shiver from the chills. He turned the car on and let the heater run. The girl was all rumpled in the way that she had sunk down in the seat, but Artie was still not inclined to move. His penis was throbbing from the pain, and he wanted to let the bleeding stop while the ice melted between his legs.

He didn't want to go anywhere. He began to realize the magnitude of what he had just done. Old, old feelings had come over him again, turning him into someone other than the passive guy who simply prepared packaged salads at the Brognia Brothers for nearby nursing homes and schools. "Poor impulse control," the psychologists had written about him in Green Haven Prison, where he had served his time for murdering that little girl fifteen years ago, and now the impulses had just killed another victim. Whatever he became at these moments, he knew as he sat there in the car, he had just put himself in trouble all over again.

He just wanted to stare at his victim, sitting with her, he remembered, for "half the night." Slowly his breathing returned to normal and slowly the chills and shivers eased. Slowly the panic and fury stopped and the demands of self-preservation pressed upon him.

He had a victim in the seat next to him. She was a whore. She wouldn't be missed. The entire front seat was stained with blood. He had to clean it. He had to get rid of this body. He had been smart enough not to kill her in the middle of Rochester. No one saw him commit the murder, and it was likely that no one saw him in the car when she got in. There were lots of cars on Lyell Avenue that night, one late-model Dodge wouldn't stand out that much. He had to get rid of the body. Then no one would suspect anything.

Finally, at around midnight, Shawcross reached over and unlocked the passenger door. He turned the ignition off and slipped out from behind the wheel on the driver's side. He opened Dorothy's side of the car and she dropped into his arms and off the seat. He picked her up and carried her across the chain that was closing the road, stepping over it so he could take her to the bridge over Salmon Creek. He carried her about thirty feet. There was no one there. Icy winds were blowing across the partially frozen stream that was already flowing slowly because of the chunks of ice. It would soon freeze over. Maybe, he thought, they wouldn't find her until the thaw. By then, who knows, he and Rose might even be in a different place.

Shawcross hefted and then dropped Dorothy Blackburn's body over the edge of the bridge, into the running water below. He heard the crack of ice and then a splash. He stood there watching the dark water for about a half hour, he told investigators, trying to pick out her facedown corpse in the darkness. Soon it would snow again and even the Dodge's tire tracks would be covered up. She was gone.

Arthur climbed back into the car and drove the fifteen or so miles back into Rochester. He drove directly over to Lake Avenue, where he had first seen Dotsie Blackburn that night and cruised the streets to see if there were police cars or anything that was not like the hundreds of other times he'd cruised through the Tent City area. He told investigators that he drove over to Mark's Coffee Shop, where he had coffee and calmed himself down.

After his arrest a year later, Rose Shawcross would tell police homicide detectives that Artie often drove into the Lake Avenue section of town early in the morning to get his newspaper and have coffee. She knew it was a bad section of town and it made her nervous that Arthur would sometimes take his bike there, but she never challenged him about it. She just let him be, she said, because he always took care of her. That was also why she didn't question him now, when he came home early in the morning and didn't tell her where he'd been or what he'd been doing.

Shawcross said that after he had his coffee and had

calmed down to where he could start thinking again, he drove to an empty parking lot where he could clean up the car without being seen. Then he collected Dorothy Blackburn's shoes, socks, and coat and took out whatever identification he could find. These he would make sure no one found. He dumped her clothing in the parking lot dumpster, again making sure that no one saw what he was doing.

He stayed with the car until daylight, he told investigators, when he could see more clearly how much blood was still in it. It was pretty bad. He remembers he cleaned it as well as he could, but he couldn't get rid of the stains. Luckily, Rose would never see the car and he could explain away any mess to Clara Neal as either fish blood or blood from some game he had tried to catch. She wouldn't know the difference. Whether the body was discovered or not, there'd be no way to trace it back to him anyway. He dropped the car off at Clara's place, picked up his bike, and rode all the way back to his studio apartment on Alexander Street. He'd make sure, he told himself, that he would stay dressed until she went to work. That way she wouldn't be able to tell how badly he was hurt and wouldn't ask any questions. Maybe his dick would heal and the scars would go away. Maybe he'd be able to clean himself up enough so that no one would notice.

No one did notice that he was hurt. He kept to himself for about a week after the murder, not saying anything to Clara, whom he didn't even see, nor to Rose. Rose attributed it to his parents' not visiting him. Clara, according to Shawcross, asked him if anything was bothering him, but he said that he never explained anything. Rose asked him what was wrong, too,

Shawcross remembers, but he didn't explain anything to her, either.

"I was in a daze for over a week," he told investigators a year later. "I felt I wasn't me, not the same me."

Shawcross said that he walked around in a fog that gradually lifted over the course of weeks. At first he felt as if he was separated from the rest of the world. He would take a long time to react to what people said or did around him. He has also described it as a kind of dream state in which another person inside of him was reacting in his place. He said he was fully conscious of what he had done, but that the murder itself was kind of misty, as if it had been more like a vivid dream than a reality.

Eventually the similarity of his life's patterns reoriented him to interacting with other people. The daily ritual of preparing the vegetables for salads at the produce company, shopping and cooking for his wife Rose, and even fishing over at Northampton Park by the creek where he had dumped Dotsie's body all helped to bring him back. The murder itself faded into the background of his consciousness. Dotsie Blackburn slipped beneath the currents and was covered over with the ice while Artie went to other fishing spots because of the frozen surface of the creek. The frozen water also helped preserve her body from decomposition for the next months. Meanwhile Arthur had awakened from his daze.

"Then I came out of the slump and didn't see another girl until April 1988. She is still alive."

Chapter 2
"Mitch"

Shawcross had applied for his New York State learner's permit, Rose told police investigators, so that he could practice for his driver's license in Clara Neal's car. Rose said she tried to dissuade him from this more than a few times because she was afraid the police would stop him and send him back to prison. She was also afraid that if he got into an accident, he'd be liable because he was an unlicensed driver. She said she also feared for his safety.

But Shawcross wanted his driver's license more than he seemed to want anything, and he told Rose that as soon as he had it he'd get rid of Clara Neal and get his own car. For the rest of February, he seemed content to drift. The frost seemed to be breaking in early March, and Shawcross began driving more and more. He still avoided fishing in Northampton Park, although as he was driving over the bridge, he noticed that the ice had broken and water was beginning to run again. He didn't seem to be afraid of being found out.

A few days after the beginning of spring, a fully clothed corpse floated to the surface of Salmon Creek near the Route 31 bridge. A hunter, venturing out onto the ice, spotted it and notified police. New York State Police from the Henrietta division along with local investigators retrieved the body and eventually made a tentative identification. She was Dorothy Blackburn, the official report said, a 27-year-old white prostitute who frequented the Lyell Avenue district of Rochester, and she had been strangled to death. "Dotsie," as her friends said she was called, was ruled a homicide victim, and the item made the local newspapers and was reported on local news broadcasts.

Rose said that she took no mind of the news of Dotsie's discovery. Art seemed a little "down," she said to police, but she didn't attribute it to the discovery of the body. "He has his moods," she said, making no connection with the Dorothy Blackburn murder. Art seemed to feel the need to go driving after the discovery, and on March 25, 1988, one day after the body was spotted, he took Clara Neal's grandchildren out in her gray 1984 Chevrolet Celebrity. A police car spotted the Chevy weaving across the center divider and pulled Shawcross over. He was ticketed for driving without a valid license and for having two unrestrained children in the backseat of the car. The police contacted Clara Neal, the car's registered owner, who identified Arthur Shawcross as her boyfriend and the children as her grandchildren.

But the investigation stopped when Clara vouched for Arthur. The police were never told that Shawcross was on probation for a manslaughter sentence and that one of the conditions of his parole, was that he was not allowed to associate with children in any way. He had been convicted originally for murdering a

29

child. Shawcross had violated his parole but was still on the loose and still able to move about freely, despite the fact that he had no driver's license and was a parole violator.

Dorothy Blackburn was one of the street hookers who the police in Rochester knew frequented the warehouse district. What she did and how she lived her life had put her outside the law and outside police protection. Kinky guys and strangers with sex hang-ups were her business. For thirty bucks she'd give you a "half-and-half" like the one she had offered Artie. No hard-on? She'd laugh in your face and take her chances. For thirty bucks you didn't have all night to get it up. But Shawcross was not just a lonely guy cruising Lyell Avenue.

Thirteen years earlier, after he had just started serving his manslaughter sentence, an anonymous psychological evaluator at Green Haven Prison in Stormville, New York, had written the words "psychopathic killer" in pencil above a typed notation stating that Shawcross appeared to be a "normal individual." The parole officers who fought his release pointed to this notation as a reason Shawcross should not be let back onto the streets. But the parole board said that he had changed, had become a model prisoner, had earned his GED and become a locksmith. They mandated psychological counseling after his release and told him he couldn't drink, spend time around children, visit prostitutes, nor carry a gun.

He'd been chased out of community after community along New York's southern tier until he was placed in Rochester. The parole board didn't even tell the cops, didn't even register him as a sex offender or a child killer. They just set him up on Alexander Street and made sure he attended his therapy sessions like the ones he attended shortly before killing Dorothy Blackburn and again after the murder. By March, however, Shawcross had turned into a new person called "Mitch," and was seen regularly cruising along Lyell Avenue looking for prostitutes and paying for his favorite "half-and-half."

There were so few clues on Dotsie Blackburn's body the police were stymied. They knew the cause of death was strangulation and not drowning, but they were also intrigued by the obvious signs of a struggle. She had not been beaten, but she was bruised across her face, and the strangulation itself had been brutal. They were also confused about the trauma to Blackburn's vagina. Had she been mutilated after death? Was it a wound that had no connection to her death? Had she received the injury during her struggle with the killer? The newspapers didn't even report that part of her vagina had actually been torn out of her, or that there were human toothmarks around the injury. Maybe they should have written it off to violent sex, but it was a part of the puzzle that investigators would hold on to until they had their suspect in custody.

On January 4, 1990, after Shawcross was in custody and was interrogated by Investigator Dennis Blythe from the New York State Police, he was asked point-blank whether he had kicked Dorothy Blackburn in the groin either in anger or to get her over the bridge embankment and into the water. "After you disposed of her, Art," Blythe asked. "Did you kick her someplace?"

"No," Shawcross answered.

"You didn't kick her in the groin area?"

"No," Shawcross said. "I just dropped her over."

In his identity as Mitch, Shawcross returned to Lake Avenue again and again. There were rumors after the death that perhaps he was dealing drugs among the prostitutes and the runaways, but that was never confirmed. Shawcross said that whenever he felt weird or broke out into a sweat after a headache, he'd start cruising in Clara's car and usually wind up in one of the bars on Lyell Avenue before he even realized where he was. With each trip, each visit to a bar, and each encounter with a prostitute, Shawcross was violating his parole. But the police never realized the extent of Shawcross's crimes because the parole board never told them about what he did.

Arthur Shawcross simply slipped beneath the surface of life, chumming for women among the warehouses and bars where Lyell Avenue intersected Lake Avenue. As long as no one saw him, as long as no one complained about him, and as long as there was no connection between Shawcross and his victims, he'd be safe. And because no more bodies turned up in Salmon Creek after Dorothy Blackburn was discovered by the hunter, the police never realized until much, much later that a serial killer was on the loose. Blackburn was listed as a prostitute homicide, and her killer could have been any one of her clients dissatisfied at the level of service he got for his thirty bucks. Or she could have been killed by a pimp who was getting her out of his way.

In April and May 1988, Arthur had two more encounters with prostitutes, but neither woman challenged him nor pushed a trigger that sent him over the edge. More than likely, whatever events sent Shawcross trolling along Lyell Avenue on those occasions passed through his consciousness quickly enough not to trip him into homicidal behavior. The last prostitute he left alive, according to his statement to investigators, was a young, skinny redhead named Ruth, who gave him oral sex in early May, took her money, and walked out into the night. She never realized that the person named Mitch in the gray Chevy was actually a psychopathic killer named Arthur Shawcross who would eventually become one of the worst serial killers in New York State history. She might still never know how close she'd come to death.

Arthur was able to control his impulses through May 1988, until two New York State Police investigators confronted Fred Brognia at his produce company and told him about the two child murders in Watertown that Shawcross had committed and served time for. Brognia fired Shawcross. He told the newspapers afterward that Shawcross had lied on his employment application when he didn't reveal the nature of his crime and that he had lied when he had told him that he'd been convicted for killing a drunken driver who'd killed his family.

Shawcross was now without a job and technically in violation of his parole. Rose had told the police that whenever he had difficulties at work, got into arguments with other people, or was reprimanded for doing something wrong, he would go into the bathroom and beat on the walls until he felt better. Then he would go fishing or ride his bike. At the very end of

May, after he was fired, Shawcross took his bike into the city, but before he had a chance to be alone, he crossed paths with his second victim.

Shawcross met prostitute Anna Steffen that day at a Lake Avenue bar in Rochester. He knew her as a street person who lived at one of the local churches but hustled on the street for whatever money she could make. He claimed to police that she solicited him, and that that was how the two of them got hooked up in the first place.

"She wanted to screw," he told investigators. He had been on his way to go fishing on an island in the Genesee River when she saw him and took him to a grassy field above the Genesee falls. "She asked for $20," he said.

Anna Steffen took off all her clothes and told Artie to join her in the water. "C'mon in, all right?" Steffen called out to Shawcross. It was a warm day.

The small island next to Driving Park Bridge was a favorite place for teenagers who wanted a quiet, deserted place to have sex. The police used to leave them pretty much alone unless they received reports of loud partying. It was also a favorite spot for runaways who had become prostitutes to take their tricks if, as with Anna Steffen, they didn't have their own place to live.

As Shawcross described it to state police detectives in January 1990, he took off his clothing and waded into the stream. The two of them started kissing and rolling around in the shallow currents. At first they tried oral sex, "oral 69," Shawcross told the investigators. "We were kissing and making out in the water and then climbed up on the embankment." That's where they had oral sex and then tried to have intercourse.

"We tried for a good forty minutes," Shawcross said. But no matter what she did or how hard he tried, he couldn't get an erection. "She tried everything."

Shawcross said that Steffen got up and pushed him into the water. Suddenly he became furious that she had turned on him, and he changed. "Something else took over. I came out of the water and gave her a shove, and she — she fell on her side."

Steffen screamed and wrenched in pain in the water as she rolled around and doubled up. "I'm going to have a baby," she said to Shawcross, who crawled back in the water after her.

"What the hell are you doing getting me to come down here and fool around if you're going to have a baby?" he hollered after her.

"I'm going to call the police," she said. "You hurt me!"

Shawcross says that he was seized with panic. He didn't have any intention of killing anybody that day, he reported. But he felt he'd been tricked by a whore who took his money, turned on him because he couldn't perform, and then, when he got angry, told him she was pregnant and threatened to call the police.

He waded out to where she was just getting up from the water and threw himself on top of her. She didn't struggle, he remembers. She didn't even try to scratch him or bite him. All two hundred and twenty pounds of him simply smothered Anna Steffen as he strangled her with both hands and held her body underwater. She died very quickly, he remembers, and he just left her there.

"I couldn't tell she was pregnant," Shawcross told police. "It was just a statement she made. She didn't

35

have no big stomach or nothing." But his fear that he had been tricked into having sex with and hurting a mother-to-be and had then been threatened with police charges that could send him back to prison made him too panicked to control any of his impulses, and he lost his instinct for self-preservation. Like an animal backed into a corner, Shawcross killed her.

He pushed her body deeper into the water and let the current take it away. He didn't even bother to conceal it in any way. He didn't bury it, didn't cover it with leaves, as he had with the little girl he'd killed fifteen years before, didn't hide it in any brushes, as he would with other bodies. He told investigators that he simply left the area after he took away her dress, "put a rock in it, and dropped it into the river."

In the warmer water Anna's body decomposed more quickly than Dotsie's, and, as with Blackburn, the police who eventually retrieved her were unable to piece together the woman's murder. They knew she'd been suffocated and drowned, they knew she'd been in the water before she died because of the amount of water in her lungs, and they knew she was a local prostitute who'd lived at the church. But Anna Steffen's body was covered with garbage, construction debris, and roofing shingles. For almost two years, the police, as State Police Lieutenant Edward Grant would tell Shawcross on January 3, 1990, the day he was arrested, believed Anna Steffen's killer had tried to camouflage his crime by covering the body with construction debris and shingles. They might even have believed that the crime was somehow related to the construction crews because of the killer's use of these materials.

At the time he killed Steffen, Shawcross remembered, there were construction crews all over Driving Park, clearing the land. Even as he and Anna were having sex in the water, Shawcross was aware of bulldozers in the distance, and earth-moving equipment. Eventually the crews would haul a dumpster to Driving Park, and as the dumping of garbage continued, a layer of garbage, twigs, scrap wood, and scrapped shingles would settle over the body of Anna Steffen as it decomposed in the river. Until Shawcross's confession, the police would not be able to relate the Steffen killing to the Blackburn killing because the bodies had been dumped so far from each other. They knew only that the two women were prostitutes.

Arthur didn't follow the stories of the discovery of Steffen's body on television. Throughout the rest of 1988, he said, he tried very hard to return to the life he was leading the year before, when he was released from prison. He even found another job working nights as a salad maker at the G & G Food Services Company over on East Main Street in Rochester. He began cruising the night spots on Lake Avenue again, but, he says, he was "okay for the rest of the year." However, beginning in 1989, he started to lead a double life as "Mitch," the Lake Avenue regular who always paid for the half-and-half, and as "Artie," the lonely guy who took extra-special care of Rose Walley Shawcross and Clara Neal, two older women who say they loved him. No one knew he was a killer, however, not even the prostitutes he was murdering, until the police announced his capture in January 1990.

Artie's third victim was not the typical "stranger murder" that has come to be associated with serial murder sprees. Unlike these "random encounter" homicides, Shawcross not only knew victim number three, he'd been intimate with her on a number of occasions, sometimes in the very apartment he shared with his wife Rose.

He'd gone down to Driving Park and over to the island, Shawcross told investigators, more to hang around and fish than to look for sex. It was June 1989. As he drove toward the bridge, he spotted 58-year-old Dorothy Keller, a homeless woman who filled in from time to time as a waitress at a diner he frequented, walking along the road toward a local mill. Dorothy Keller was also a potential girlfriend, one of Shawcross's confidants, who knew Rose, and who'd been to the apartment. Dorothy had no address, Shawcross told police. She'd lived over at the Oxford Catholic Church on Monroe Avenue.

"We had an affair," Shawcross confessed to Investigator Dennis Blythe. "And she'd come to the house a lot. We stayed there a few times and she started stealing money and stuff out of the house and I told her about it. And she says, 'Nothing you can do about it because I will tell your wife.' I said 'All right.' " Shawcross had decided to live with what was going on because they were "friends," and he didn't want to upset the status quo. Dorothy Keller also fit the profile of Shawcross's other stable relationships, with Rose Walley Shawcross and Clara Neal. All three were older women who mothered Shawcross and whom he had trusted.

Shawcross did not refer to Dorothy Keller as a prostitute when he confessed to murdering her. He referred to her only as a waitress friend of his from the neighborhood and a woman with whom he was having an affair. From the description of their relationship he gave authorities, it seemed Keller was more dependent upon Shawcross for sex and affection than he was upon her. He told Lieutenant Grant that he and Dorothy had also frequently gone down to the river, where they "fooled around" and "goofed around" on the island, having oral sex and intercourse. She would have become his third relationship had she not confronted and threatened him on that June afternoon in 1989.

After she noticed Clara Neal's car passing her on the road, and Arthur all puffed up behind the wheel and steering with his arms straight out, she asked him where he was going.

"Down to the island," he yelled out of the window, "to fish."

"I'm coming, too," Dorothy called out, and Artie opened the passenger door and let her in.

They drove down to the island, where he set up his rod and tackle, but "we didn't get no fishing done," Artie later told Dennis Blythe. "We just screwed around in the park."

Shawcross said that he and Dorothy Keller never had any problem having sexual intercourse. He trusted her. And on that day there was no reason to be afraid of anything — at first. "We made love okay," he said, "and goofed off the morning." About 1 P.M. it started to rain, and Artie found an old discarded blanket which he set up as a makeshift tent over a few limbs from trees that were being trimmed back by someone who "was sawing trees down there."

As they sat there under the blanket with the rain running off, Artie confronted Dorothy Keller about her

39

stealing his "laundry money" on the days during the previous winter when she'd stay at the Shawcross apartment while Rose was at work. "I asked her why she had to steal the quarters I had for laundry. I'd give her money each week — why steal?"

He told police that Keller would steal food from the apartment as well, and that it made him mad because she worked in a diner and had access to all the food she wanted. It was as if as hard as Arthur Shawcross had tried to add Dorothy Keller to the Rose Walley/Clara Neal category of older women he could trust, she had breached that trust. She stole from him.

Artie and Dorothy ate lunch under the blanket in the warm June rain and bickered about the money until Dorothy said that she was going to tell Rose that she and Arthur had made love in Rose's very own bed. Arthur said that he reeled at first from the shock.

"I sat there on a rock to think on how to stop this," he revealed later. "I asked Dorothy why she would do this. She stated she wanted me all for herself. I told her, 'No, we can't do that.' Then she said that she can tell the cops that I raped her."

Shawcross was in complete shock. He told investigators that they had been having an affair for months, that she had come over to the house the previous year, that he'd given her money to tide her over some of the rough spots between paychecks at the diner, and that they'd just gotten finished having sex and it had actually been fun. He considered her a friend and a confidant. And now, she told him, she was going to get him in trouble with the police. He'd lose Rose for sure, he thought. He'd lose Clara. And more than likely he'd probably have to go back to jail. Then there was no telling what would happen if the police put two and two together and figured out he'd already committed two murders. He'd never see the outside of prison again.

Artie looked around and saw all the logs that had been cut the previous few days. "I took a piece of cut log," he told investigators, "and I hit her on the side of the head. I think I broke her neck. She died instantly."

Arthur carried Dorothy Keller to a downed tree in high grass and hid her body there. It was tall brush, he told both Blythe and Grant. He moved her, he told the police, so that the body wouldn't be discovered, even by passersby or workmen cutting trees for the construction. With the body in the tall grass, Arthur said, it was as if she was out of sight and out of mind. No one would discover it.

After the murder, he went down to the mill in the direction that Dorothy was originally going and talked to the people who were fishing down there. He didn't feel strange, he said, nor did he feel as if anything was out of the ordinary. His only concern was that he'd murdered her at one of his favorite fishing spots and that the body might be discovered. He returned to the spot a few days later, but, he said, he didn't even check on the body. He had left it fully clothed and concealed off the road in the high grass, but had done nothing else. And as the summer wore on, it became obvious to him that she would remain undisturbed.

"About three months went by," he told investigators later, "and I went down there about 6 A.M. and used a stick to take the skull and toss it into the river. I don't know why I did not take the rest of the bones and do the same." Still, he added, she continued to decom-

41

pose in that spot all summer long. "There was this smell, but no one wanted to check it out."

Dorothy Keller's body was finally discovered, however, by fishermen and construction workers who reported the headless corpse to the police. By now Keller had been reported missing for six months, but no one had made the connection between Shawcross, who had probably been seen driving her from the diner to the island and at whose apartment she might have been seen, and the lonely waitress. It was as if Arthur Shawcross had pulled a camouflage netting over himself so completely that even when he walked among the corpses of his own victims, people—including the police—took no notice. This became apparent to Lieutenant Grant when he asked Shawcross about the discovery of Keller's corpse.

Arthur had told the state police investigators that he was standing right there when the police discovered the body. For him, going to the island at Driving Park was "business as usual" because he fished there so often.

"Didn't the police talk to you when they found the body?" Lieutenant Grant asked Shawcross in January 1990, after his arrest.

"Nope," Shawcross answered. "I was down there all the time, so there was no reason to ask me anything."

Shawcross followed the news of Keller's discovery on television and in the local papers and saw the crime tape marking off the spot where the corpse was found. He said that he felt no remorse over the crime and didn't have any reason to let the police know—even anonymously—that she had been killed. He said that even though they had been friends, once she was killed, his only concern was that the body not be found right away and that he himself not be connected to the disappearance or the discovery of the corpse in any way.

The police did not, at first, tie the Keller murder to the Blackburn or Steffen homicides, even though Steffen was discovered in the same general area just a few months later. According to typical investigatory procedures, Keller didn't fit into the Blackburn and Steffen profiles. Blackburn was discovered miles away from Keller and Steffen; Keller was found headless and in tall grass on land rather than in the water; and Steffen, the police assumed, had been camouflaged with construction debris and roofing shingles. Although both Blackburn and Steffen had suffocated, Steffen had water in her lungs from drowning during the struggle for her life; Blackburn had been dead at least four hours prior to being dumped in the icy stream.

The Keller homicide fit neither profile, because the victim had a broken neck and had not been strangled. She was more fully decomposed than either Blackburn or Steffen, and the police didn't have a skull to use to determine the victim's identity. She was also too old to fit into the profile of the two earlier victims. What no one knew, until after Arthur Shawcross had confessed, was that the basic similarities between Steffen and Keller had only to do with the threats both women posed to Arthur Shawcross. He had said that when they told him they were going to complain to the police that they had been raped, he was seized by fear and murdered them to protect himself.

The police were also stymied by the three homicides because there were so few clues on the victims, who did not seem to have put up any struggle. It looked, at the very first, like these were three unrelated crimes that could have been solved by traditional investigatory procedures. No one was yet saying that a serial killer was on the loose in Rochester and, indeed, according to Arthur Shawcross's own confessions, the three killings weren't "stranger" murders at all. He had known Steffen well before he'd killed her — he had known that she was a homeless runaway who stayed at the local parish — and the Keller homicide was a fight between lovers. Keller had no reason to fear Shawcross, she thought, because she had been controlling him for months with the threat of telling Rose that they were having an affair. In fact, according to Arthur's confession, Keller's motive was not money or food, but control. She said that she didn't want to share Artie with two other women. If he is to be believed, she acted out of panic and desperation at losing his affections and he acted out of panic and desperation at the disclosure of his affair. It is no wonder that the police were unable to assign the same killer profile to all three homicides.

In each and every case, however, Shawcross himself has said it was an aggressive act on the part of the victim that turned him into someone not himself. He said it when Dorothy Blackburn bit into his penis so hard that he thought he was critically injured, when Anna Steffen told him she was going to the police to file a charge that she'd been raped and injured during pregnancy, and when Dorothy Keller told him that not only was she going to tell Rose and Clara, she was filing rape charges as well. In each case something came over him that made him kill without thinking. He said he had had no intention of killing when he had first seen each victim. That was the reason that he was able to

44

have dealings with many prostitutes without committing more murders, and also, the reason that the women themselves had no idea Shawcross was a murderer.

It was that lack of prehomicidal volition on his part that made detection so difficult. Not even the victims knew they were victims until he had assaulted them. These were not typical serial "lust" homicides at all, but a series of "traditional" homicides between friends or lovers. It stymied the police for two full years as Shawcross began his rampage. Even later, in 1989, police investigators told newspapers that the unidentified killer was so much in control of each victim and crime scene that they believed the killer was using a "stun gun" to disable the victims first.

But Arthur Shawcross wasn't finished. As he became more deeply enmeshed in the web and terror of his own crimes, he became even more dangerous. He wooed every woman who crossed his path, but the minute she turned on him or threatened him in any way, Shawcross killed her as if she were an insect, disposed of the corpse, and walked away from it as if it were business as usual.

Patty Ives would be next.

Chapter 3
"I Know Who You Are"

Shawcross had already known Patty Ives from the Lake Avenue neighborhood. She had seen Shawcross ride through the neighborhood on his bike, and the two of them had begun talking. They didn't do anything with each other, Art said; they just talked while he leaned on his bike and listened to her tell him about who she was doing tricks with and what she wanted for sex. Artie didn't have any money on him, he said, but he told her that he'd be back in a couple of days with money for a half-and-half. This was on a Wednesday.

"I said that I got paid on Friday and I would have to pay whatever bills I had," he told police. "I also had to buy food and groceries for Rose, and then, if I had anything left over, I'd buy fishing equipment."

Three days later, Shawcross showed up on schedule, meeting her by the unclaimed freight building on Lake Avenue, near the Princess Diner, where he had often seen Dorothy Keller. "I rode down to Driving Park and fished for a few hours. I went back up on top of the bridge and crossed over toward Lake Avenue and went over to the Princess Diner when a girl hollered at me. That was Patty Ives."

"Let's go have sex," Patty said, according to Shawcross in his statement to Investigator Blythe.

"For how much money?" Blythe asked Shawcross, intrigued by the ease with which Shawcross seemed to pick up his victims.

"We didn't discuss money then," Shawcross said. "We just went to do it. We went behind the fence at the rear of the YMCA, where there's a whole bed of soft sod near some construction where somebody'd been digging up the area. It's like a bed of dirt back there. Patty led me to a spot under the tree where they couldn't see us."

Artie said he put his bike behind a tree where no one would steal it and Patty led him to the dirt bed she'd prepared. "I gave her $25 as all I had," Shawcross said. "She took her black pants down, put one leg out so's I could get in, and pulled up her shirt. She gave me regular sex. While I was on top of her she was rubbing my back and legs. We were kissing also."

Shawcross felt Patty's hands running over his back and around his buttocks. Then he felt her hand pull something out of his back pocket and try to jam it back in again, but it got caught in the folds. It was his wallet. "She had taken all the money out of the wallet, then tried to put my wallet back. I grabbed her arms, took back my money, and took back the $25 I'd given her. Then I told her we'd continue doing what we came here to do." It was more of an order than a suggestion, Shawcross said, as he began pumping up and down on her as hard as he could.

There were children playing at a nearby park, and

Shawcross believed they were too close. He and Patty would be seen. Patty started groaning as the two of them began having intercourse. Shawcross told her to be quiet. "Keep it down," he kept hissing in her ear. "Those kids'll know what we're doing and come over." They kept arguing about the kids while he "kept on pumping and trying to come." "I didn't have no trouble having sex with her," Artie told investigators. "I just couldn't have an orgasm."

Then, he said, Patty started crying. He told her to stop crying or else he would have to "shut her up." She said through tears that she wanted him to stop because he was hurting her. But Shawcross said that he kept right on pumping as hard as he could because he wanted to have an orgasm.

"Patty got mad then, and told me who I was," Shawcross told investigators. "She told me that she had seen me and Anna Steffen together down in the field by Driving Park, and that she and Anna used to take their johns down there for business. Then Patty tried to get out from under me. I grabbed her legs and reentered her but hit her asshole instead. Suddenly that felt good and I couldn't stop. She screamed, but I put my hand over her mouth. Then, as I pulled out, I had my orgasm. Then I was kissing her. Then I put my hand over her mouth and lay on top of her with my hand on her throat as she fought and wiggled to get out from under. But she couldn't. I was strangling her and having sex with her at the same time, and she was taking a long time to die."

Finally Patty stopped struggling and trying to kick her way out from under the heavier Shawcross. She was dead. Arthur said that he put her leg back in the pant leg and pulled up her pants. Then he pulled down her blouse. He dragged her over to the fence and into the brush where there was a deep depression in the ground. He noticed there was a wide wooden board resting against the fence, and he placed it on top of Patty's body. He told Lieutenant Grant that it didn't matter to him whether the victim's body was face up or facedown, mouth open or mouth closed, dressed or undressed. He was only trying to conceal the body so that by the time someone discovered it, he would have long left the scene and wouldn't be associated with the crime.

Shawcross also said that he had lost all track of time during the actual murder what with his having had an orgasm for the first time in a long while. "I was soaking wet from sweating and didn't hear anything around me," he said. The noise of the children and passing trucks had been completely obliterated by the emotional energy of the homicide itself. "I couldn't figure that out," he said, "plus, the day was much brighter. That was scary, like I was all alone in that whole area. I picked up my wallet and sat there until dark. Then went home."

Arthur Shawcross said that by the time he got home he had returned to normal. He had no remorse for Patty Ives, although he did feel that he had escaped detection because he had killed a possible connecting witness to the Anna Steffen murder. Maybe he realized that he had not been quite so invisible after all. If Patty Ives had been able to identify him as one of Steffen's johns, and if other prostitutes in the area knew that he had been friendly with Patty Ives for months before her death, he might be connected to the homicides.

Rumors of a prostitute killer in Rochester were already circulating among the hookers in the Lake Avenue area, and Shawcross had heard stories of women who were afraid to do the streets for fear of being picked up turning a trick and then killed. But the police were yet to go public with any real information about the killings.

On a chilly fall evening two months after he killed Patty Ives, Shawcross met Frances Brown standing at the corner of Lake and Ambrose Avenues. Shawcross was driving Clara's Dodge Omni again when Frances stepped out into the street to stop the person she knew as Mitch.

"How much?" Shawcross asked as she slipped into the seat alongside Artie.

"We'll talk about that when we get there," she said. "Drive."

Shawcross said that they started off toward Driving Park (it had become almost a ritual for him by now), but that they turned left after they crossed the bridge and drove along Seth Green Drive toward one of the Kodak factories along the Genesee River. They pulled into a parking lot behind one of the buildings and Frances turned to Shawcross and demanded thirty dollars. "Mitch" handed over the money and leaned over the front seat to drop the rear seats while she took off all her clothing except her socks.

"We started doing oral 69," Shawcross said, "but then she went wild and somewhat crazy. She didn't act right. She asked me to 'deep throat' her, so I did."

But Shawcross said that he got carried away and pressed his penis into her throat so deep that she couldn't breathe. She went into convulsions, he said, and "I couldn't stop, and she peed into my mouth as I kept pushing." She stopped moving. Then she stopped breathing. But Shawcross didn't stop. He said he kept on doing it to her even after she had died, using her "while she was still warm, even kissing her and sucking her tongue and breast. I didn't have an orgasm."

Shawcross said that he pulled up his pants and sat next to her in the car for about an hour while he listened to a local country-and-western station on the car radio. He felt he could have waited there all night if he'd wanted to because the area was deserted. It was right next to a deep gorge where area fishermen would pull out tables during the day to gut and filet their fish. At night they would lower the tables over the edge of the gorge. Shawcross had fished there many times, he said, and he knew that there would be no one out there at night.

Finally, at about midnight, he got out of the car and opened the door on the passenger side. He dragged Frances Brown's body along the front seat and rolled it out of the car and over the embankment into the gorge. As he watched it tumble, he told police the following year, he saw how it gathered debris on the way down, effectively camouflaging it from the top of the gorge, unless you knew where it was. When the police discovered the body, they'd thought at first that the killer had deliberately tried to cover up the body with debris. Shawcross told them that the whole thing had happened while she scraped along the edge of the embankment.

The last thing about Frances Brown that Shawcross remembered was the way she landed on the bottom. "She was butt-up," he said almost without emotion.

"Butt-up right in the air. And I see'd the tattoo she had on her butt. Was the last I ever saw of her. The tattoo said, 'Kiss off.' And that's exactly what she'd done."

Then he drove back to Shaheen Paints on St. Paul Street, where he took all of Frances Brown's clothing and threw it in the dumpster behind the building. Arthur knew that the clothing wouldn't stay there for long. Haulers came every morning before sunup to take the day's garbage, and by the time anyone discovered the girl's body, her clothing would be on its way to the transfer station and from there to the landfill. It was likely that no one would ever find her belongings.

Then he went home, he said, and didn't think about Frances Brown even after the police had discovered her body and he'd read about it in the newspaper.

"Weren't you even anxious when you heard about the reports of the body's discovery on television?" Lieutenant Grant asked Shawcross during his interrogation.

"Nope," he answered. "It was just like it was business as usual."

The Frances Brown murder marked the beginning of an escalation of homicides and violence for Arthur Shawcross. The death of the fifth area prostitute in just over eighteen months, the similarities in the ways the bodies were dumped in remote wooded areas or left under brushes or twigs, and the central Lake Avenue connection of all the victims led the police to believe for the first time that they might have a serial killer who was targeting prostitutes he picked. However, the murder of June Stottss just a couple of weeks later, in the first week of November, though similar to the earlier killings, had so many marked differences that the police soon thought they had two or three different killers working the area.

By this time news of the "Rochester Nightstalker," the "Rochester Strangler," or the "Genesee River Killer" had begun to make headlines on the New York metropolitan television news. There were enough similarities to the Green River prostitute murders in Seattle or the San Diego stranglings in California to suggest to some authorities that the same killer had committed all the crimes. Then, when news of a New Bedford, Massachusetts, serial killer broke into the news, other authorities speculated that the same killer was at work.

Different experts offered different theories about the killings, but still no one at the state division of parole or the state police went public with the news that a recently paroled killer was now living in the city of Rochester. Even though the state police had known of Shawcross's whereabouts and the local police had been told that a murderer had been paroled in the city, no one seemed to want to check on Shawcross's activities. Had they done so, and had they interviewed witnesses who had seen him with some of the women he eventually strangled, it is possible that Shawcross's sixth victim might have been spared. June Stotts was another local neighborhood character. She was a mildly retarded young woman who had been a regular friend of both Artie's and Rose's.

June Stotts had always told Artie that her name was "Jay," Shawcross told investigators just two months later. She had been to the Shawcross apartment so many times for lunch and dinner that Artie and Rose felt she was like one of the family. "She wasn't a hooker," Shawcross said after he was arrested. He said he'd first met her in a place called Midtown back in 1988 and had become friendly with her. Every once in a while they'd have coffee together at the local Dunkin' Donuts and he'd invite her over to the house for dinner.

On an unseasonably warm November day, Shawcross saw June Stotts sitting on a park bench near the river and asked her if she wanted to come along for a ride. The two drove down to one of the beaches along the river where they could see the barges being towed in and out of their slips, and they fed the gulls and pigeons with a loaf of bread that Shawcross had in the back of Clara's car.

"We walked hand-in-hand along the piers," Shawcross said, describing the encounter as a romantic interlude. "When we were walking along the boat dock she kissed me. Why, I don't know."

They bought some more bread from a nearby grocery store and drove to a park called Turning Point, where there was a lookout point that jutted out into the river. They sat down on the concrete pier and began throwing more pieces of bread out to the birds flocking around them, and June kissed him again. He says that he pulled her close in an embrace and asked her where she'd learned to kiss like that.

"From watching TV," Jay said.

Shawcross said that a light suddenly went on in him. "I was smitten," he said months later.

They walked hand-in-hand back to what Shawcross describes as a "cinder road" by a pier where a barge was tied up. He found an old gray rug there and spread it out like a picnic blanket. They sat back on it and Artie took off his coat, rolled it up, and used it as a pillow for his head. "Jay" Stotts leaned over him and kissed him a third time. Then, as she sat there watching him, Shawcross remembered, a concerned look came over her face. Shawcross told Investigator Blythe that Jay told him she'd never had sex before, that she was a virgin. "She asked me if I would show her how to do certain things." He said he explained how men and women made love and she took off her pants and shirt, laid them on the ground, and then took Shawcross's pants off.

"We was sitting touching each other," Shawcross continued. "And I was showing her, and got down to intercourse, and I told her, I says, 'For a girl that says she never had sex before, it went in pretty easy, no blood or nothing.' I said, 'You ain't no virgin.' "

That was when she seemed to turn into a different person, Shawcross told Blythe. "She started screaming; she says, 'I am going to tell, I am going to tell.' "

"Tell what?" Blythe asked Shawcross during his interrogation.

"Tell everybody we were having sex down there. And I put my hand over her mouth, stopping her from screaming and hollering," Shawcross answered, and he explained that he suffocated her.

Months after his initial interrogation, Shawcross wrote down a different story for medical investigators writing a report for the defense team. In this later version, he said that he *assumed* June Stotts was a virgin because she had asked him to teach her how to make love. But he was puzzled, he remembered, because he thought that she was at least thirty years old.

Shawcross says he took off all his clothes and lay

down beside her. "I kissed her and ran my hand over her body. No response at all. Kissed her neck and breast, her stomach also. Took off her underpants and she closed her eyes. She was a funny girl. Gave her oral sex. Nothing happened. So I laid next to her with one leg between her legs, looked in her eyes, and kissed her. She did not know how to French-kiss. But something was wrong. I kept looking at her and stroking her vagina. Her eyes showed me nothing. Then we talked. She never had a man. Jay had been with women."

Shawcross said he was perplexed at first, but he mounted her and tried to have intercourse.

"She screamed, and then fainted. I was in then. Stayed in till she came to. Then I screw her for a good twenty minutes, fast and slow. I couldn't stop, it felt that good. Then she started. She went wild on me. Couldn't get enough, seems like. When I got tired, she tried to keep me up. Jay was not Jay at that moment. She turned into something else. Wild, crazy. How can I explain? She used my hands, toes, and face. I could not stop her. She used her hands, both at the same time. Then she sucked me. I gave her more. I thought that I had come. So did she. Then she sat up and said she was going to tell the police I raped her. I snapped once again. It was over in ten minutes."

He said that he left Stotts lying right where he'd killed her, in a deserted spot of the shoreline near where the barges tied up. He took her clothing and dropped them right in the river next to the barges and watched as they sank to the bottom. He took her knife with him, though; it was a little pocketknife with a three-to-four-inch blade that locked open. "I kind of liked it," he said. He put it in his pocket when he left the body lying by the shore.

A week later, just before sunrise, Shawcross took the bus back to the spot near where he'd killed Stotts. He walked to where her body lay and found that she was undisturbed. He said he sat there next to her for a while and just watched her. He found her glasses and some change from her pocket nearby and threw them in the swampy water along the shore so that there were no identifying articles. Then he said he felt the body. "It was warm," he said. "It was limp. So I screwed her some more. Then I took out the knife that I'd taken from her and cut her wide open in a straight line down her chest from, her neck to her asshole. Cut out her pussy and ate it. I was one sick person. Dragged her into the swamp, then put the rug over her and left."

Artie explained to state police investigators that he hadn't cut June Stotts open because he hated her or even because he hated his crime. He said he felt nothing about his crime, not even remorse. Actually, he explained to both Dennis Blythe and Ed Grant, he'd actually liked June Stotts. He cut her open, he said, only so that she would decompose quicker after he'd dragged her into the swampy water. Then he laid the underside of the rug over her so that she would be hidden from view once she was in the tall grass and rushes.

Shawcross had learned how to use a knife and how to dress game from his experience as a deer hunter. He also knew about eviscerating animals from his experience as a meat cutter at a meat packing plant up in Watertown, New York. It was in Watertown that he'd had his first taste of raw flesh and blood, a taste that, he said, remained with him through Vietnam and now in Rochester.

The police had tried to get Shawcross to talk about the marks on June Stotts and the organs he'd cut out of her, but Shawcross didn't mention it to investigators until months later. It wouldn't be until a series of blood tests and urine analyses were conducted on him by labs at SmithKline Beecham and Norsom that doctors would discover a chemical aberration known as kryptopyrroluria combined with a severe vitamin B_6 deficiency which rendered Shawcross not only incapable of controlling his violent urges under emotional pressure, but made him a medical cannibal. He is one of the first serial killers ever to have been so diagnosed.

Chapter 4
Feeding Frenzy

By the time the local police had announced the discovery of June Stotts' body in the swampy backwaters by the industrial piers in the factory section along the river, the newspapers were besieging them for answers about Rochester's own Jack the Ripper. Was he the same mysterious stalker who had been strangling local prostitutes since 1988? Was he the same one who had killed a number of black prostitutes in the Lake Avenue area? Was he the same person who had sliced open June Stotts' corpse from neck to crotch? If the police were focusing on a prostitute killer, local commentators were saying, then the June Stotts murder might be unrelated to the others. If the killer was white, why would he murder black prostitutes? There was another theory that the murder of Dorothy Blackburn, whose body was found all the way over in Northampton Park in Salmon Creek, might not even be related to the other slayings.

Newspaper reporters demanded clues, daily press briefings, updates on the investigation, insights into the mind of the killer who was dumping these victims, and information about what the police were doing to apprehend him. Gradually Rochester became a mecca for television journalists and segment producers from the tabloid news shows. Everywhere you looked, another camera crew was shooting background footage of the Genesee River piers where the bodies had been dumped and Driving Point Park. The prostitutes themselves were also sought out for interviews. "Did you know Anna Steffen?" "Was Dotsie a regular on this street?" "Are you afraid for your own life?" "How often do the police patrol down here?" "Any strange people cruising through the neighborhood lately?" No one mentioned Mitch. No one talked about a guy in a blue-gray Dodge Omni or in a gray Chevrolet Celebrity who had been the last person to see some of the victims alive.

The New York City daily newspapers were also describing the peculiarities of the case and asking whether Rochester had its own version of Seattle's Green River Killer or whether a number of killers were attacking prostitutes in Rochester. The Lake Avenue streetwalkers themselves had begun to get scared. Many of them had known Patty Ives, Anna Steffen, Dotsie Blackburn, and Dorothy Keller. Yet they didn't connect the deaths of these women with the kindly-looking middle-aged man named Mitch who drove through the neighborhood and solicited women for oral sex.

There were at least three women, including the redhead named Ruthie, who'd invested time in trying to help Mitch get an erection to no avail. Mitch had made them promise when they started that if he couldn't get an erection or have an orgasm because he had "problems," he wouldn't owe them anything. At least three women went for the deal and refunded him his $25. They lived to try again. Those women who wouldn't refund his money, who laughed at him, who threatened him, or who made him angry in any way were strangled.

Through the final months of 1989, fresh bodies began turning up in area parks and streams with alarming regularity. These corpses were hardly decomposed. They had been recently killed and recently dumped. That meant that not only was the killer still killing in his same territory, he was actively hunting for prey while the police were trying to determine who he was and how he was attracting his victims. The increase in the number of bodies also meant that the killer was on a feeding frenzy, according to the local newspapers, killing with impunity while the police tried to find the clue that would bring him in. The more bodies that turned up, the more it seemed as if the killer was operating right under the noses of the patrols blanketing the neighborhood. But they still couldn't catch him because he was blending into the local population too well and the case itself was totaling up to a big zero while the television crews and newspaper photographers rushed from site to site with the discovery of each new body.

In November, Arthur Shawcross cruised along Lake Avenue to pick up Maria Welch his seventh victim. In his statement to police the day after he was arrested, Shawcross said she climbed into Clara's Dodge Omni and they drove down to the end of Lake Avenue where it meets with Dewey Avenue at a little beach facing the lake. Then the two started bargaining.

"I get $25 for oral, $40 for regular, and $35 for half-and-half."

"Well, you know, I'll give you $20 for oral," Shawcross said.

Welch began hollering at him, Shawcross said. She screamed that that was not what she expected, she wanted more; why was she wasting her time with him when she could be making some real money back up the street?

"Hey, lady," Shawcross growled back, "you should have told me what you wanted when we were back downtown."

So she took the twenty, Shawcross told the cops, then she said, "Hey, I'll tell you what, I'll give you regular sex and you give me $25, right?"

Shawcross handed over an additional five dollars.

He said that he kept his pants on and unzipped his fly while Maria Welch wrapped her legs around him and slipped her hand into his back pocket while they were having intercourse. She took his wallet out of his pocket, emptied it on the seat beside her, and slipped it back into his pocket while she continued to grind. Shawcross said that while he was moving, he felt that the wallet was half out of his pants. When he "got all done," he reached back, opened his wallet, and found that it was empty.

"Give me back the money and the papers," he demanded.

"Not before I get what I want," she said.

"That's when I grabbed her and choked her," he said to the cops.

Months later, Shawcross told medical investigators

that he'd had a different reason for killing Maria Welch.

The November chill had already settled over Rochester, he remembered, and when he picked up the girl, she was cold and shivering. They just sat in the car for a while while he ran the heater on high. They didn't haggle over money at all. He simply handed over thirty dollars and she took off all her clothing.

"I asked her if she was on the rag and she said no, but when I put my hand in her, I felt a Tampax and blood. I've never done it that way. I asked for my money back. She told me to go fuck myself. I choked her until she passed out. I had some rope in the car and tied her hands behind her, plus her feet to her hands. I took out the Tampax and pushed in a bar towel. She came to and asked me what I did to her. Then she wanted me to untie her. I was sweating like crazy. Kept wiping my head and face off. I pulled out that bar towel and it was almost clean. Then I mounted her. My sweat kept dripping onto her face. That was when she said, 'I love you.' I kissed her and then killed her."

Shawcross said that he took Maria Welch's body down to a place near Island Cottage Road and Seth Green Drive where he untied her and carried her into a thick clump of bushes and trees. He sat her up on the ground so that she looked directly out onto the waters of the Genesee River. Then he went back to the car and drove to nearby Russell Station, where he rolled Welch's clothes around a rock and tied them into a ball with the rope and threw it into Long Pond. It sank to the bottom, he remembered, while he stood there staring into the dark waters as echoes of the splash died away in the night. He didn't think about Maria Welch again.

On November 11, police found the body of Frances Brown in the Genesee River gorge. There was a cold drizzle on that gray Saturday as the police crime lab unit deployed on the riverbank while the body was fished out. Both Frances Brown and Patricia Ives had been killed by strangulation. There were at least two other prostitutes who had been killed by strangulation and whose bodies had turned up in the gorge. Other women had been found in Salmon Creek, and there were still more listed as missing. Now police were convinced that they had the evidence to tie at least one serial killer to the strangulation murders of the white prostitutes in addition to two or more individual killers who had killed old women and black prostitutes. In addition there were the drug murders, the shootings, and the stabbings.

By now the Rochester police had sixty full-time city detective investigators assigned to the serial crimes unit and had established a "serial investigators only" war room on the fourth floor of the Rochester Public Safety Building. They compiled thousands of tips and clues—most of which led to dead ends and blind alleys—and had interviewed fifty suspects. No one knew about Shawcross yet. No one working in the serial killer unit had been told that the New York State Parole Board had placed a convicted multiple killer, arsonist, and sex offender in the community and had provided him with anonymity while allowing him to establish a new life.

The detectives in the serial killer unit had been debating whether a single killer was on the loose or whether there was no serial killer at all, only a weird set of circumstances that appeared to relate individual prostitute murders. The first few corpses had been discovered between the summer and early autumn months of 1989. But within the past few weeks of October and early November the discovery of multiple corpses in the Genesee River gorge revealed obvious patterns to the police. The majority of the victims were young white women who had been working as prostitutes and who had been strangled. None of the prostitute murders had been witnessed, and the early bodies were so badly decomposed that there were no usable clues.

Finally when fresh bodies began turning up only days after the victims had been reported missing, the police began hoping they were close enough to the killer that increased surveillance in the area might open up some leads. Rochester's Deputy Chief of Police Terrence M. Rickard had been quoted as saying that in the backs of the investigators' minds, they believed they had a serial killer out there. However, they were still hoping that there were enough dissimilarities to discount the possibility. By the time Brown's body was discovered in November, though, the police knew they were in the serial-murder phase of their investigation. As long as the bodies kept turning up fresh, they also knew that the killer was very close and the investigation might be near its end.

"The common strain is prostitution and a heavy addiction to cocaine," Deputy Police Chief Terrence M. Rickard said in statements to the press. "We believe there could be links to five possibly six, of the cases. We have killers—two, three, maybe four we're looking for." The police knew that the amount of cocaine being trafficked in the area and the number of local prostitutes who were addicted to drugs was forcing them to take chances they wouldn't normally take. Women were working alone at hours of the morning when they were easy prey to anyone looking for violent sex. Women in the area were putting themselves into the hands of strangers simply for a handful of bills to buy them their next bag of crack.

Even the prostitutes themselves had begun to criticize their own practices and had begun to form surveillance teams and a "buddy system" to keep eyes on one another's backs. One woman told the newspapers that she had a friend who hired a guy to stand on the corner of Lake and Lyell Avenues every time she walked the streets. The guy was taking down license plate numbers and descriptions of cars, the ex-hooker said, and if the woman wasn't back in a half hour, the guy was supposed to call the cops and give them information on the car.

The women described victims such as Patty Ives and Dorothy Blackburn who were well known in the area. One prostitute said that 25-year-old Patty Ives was a friend of hers with a terrible drug addiction. "When you're feeding the habit," she told the *New York Times*, "and my friend Patty did have one, you get desperate and the coke takes the fear away. You feel you can handle anything that's going to come."

Chief Rickard admitted that the police were particularly puzzled by the murder of June Stotts because she wasn't a prostitute, she was mildly retarded, and her abduction, as far as the police understood it, did not fit into the pattern of the other abductions and murders. "She didn't even like to ride in a car with family members," Chief Rickard said in a statement to the press. "She walked everywhere."

When the police found June Stotts' decomposing body on November 23, they said that it bore no sign of a struggle. Rickard said it was a mystery to him how she might have been lured into the killer's car. He also said that he couldn't determine exactly how or why the killer had murdered her. Rickard didn't reveal that June Stotts had been cut open from her neck to her vagina or that she had been sexually mutilated. She was the only victim who had been cut in that way, which also placed her outside the police's victim profile and suggested that she might not have been killed by the same person who had murdered the prostitutes. The police did not know that June was a friend of both Arthur Shawcross and Rose Walley Shawcross and had frequently been seen with Shawcross at a local restaurant. The police had not been told that Shawcross was a paroled killer.

Less than two weeks after June Stotts' body was discovered, Arthur Shawcross met his next victim, Darlene Trippi, whom he picked up late one afternoon in early December. He told investigators Bill Barnes and Len Borriello on January 4, 1990, that there was no snow on the ground yet, but that he knew that Christmas was coming. He was sitting in Clara's rented Dodge in Daus Alley when Darlene walked up and asked him if he wanted a date.

"Possibly," he told her, and she climbed in the car and shivered from the cold.

They drove, Shawcross told the police, and kept on driving through warehouse parking lot after warehouse parking lot across Dewey Avenue, where he'd met Maria Welch, until they came to an expanse of truck parking areas along Emerson Avenue. Trippi evidently knew that these would be empty and isolated at that time of day. She directed Shawcross to drive the car behind three tractor trailers that were angled in toward the back wall of a loading dock and hadn't been moved out of the parking lot for a few months. They wouldn't be disturbed there, she told him.

"I gave her thirty dollars for half-and-half," Shawcross told the police, "but I wasn't getting an orgasm."

He said that he told her she wasn't any good because she couldn't get him to get an erection. "She was playing with it and playing with it and says, 'You're hopeless.' And I got mad. I was embarrassed. I told her to shut up. She called me a little boy and baby-talked at me."

Shawcross said that he tried to take his money back and grabbed her to force it out of her hand. She grabbed him by the ears to get him to let her go. Shawcross said he pushed hard against her chin, forcing it against her neck and forcing her against the car door. He kept pressing, choking off her airway by pressing her chin into her neck and pushing her head against the door so she couldn't wriggle free. He kept pressing until she stopped moving. Then he pressed some more until her breathing stopped. He waited, sitting beside her in the early evening darkness, sweat pouring off him onto her body, until he felt the chill in the air reach him again. By then he was calming down and the identity that was Darlene Trippi was fading into the blur of the identities of his other victims.

Arthur carefully undressed Darlene's body, making

sure to remove all identifying jewelry and items of clothing. He drove the body to an isolated location on North Redman Road near Brockport, where he left it exposed in the woods. "Then I dump her clothes in the Salvation Army boxes on Monteu Road and 104." Trippi's clothes would have not looked any different from the hundreds of articles donated by people to the Salvation Army and might well have never been located had not Shawcross been caught less than a month later.

The "freshness" of Trippi's corpse, her similar victim profile — she was a known prostitute from the Lake Avenue area — and the death resulting from strangulation told police that the serial killer they were looking for was only a few steps ahead of them. When they found her body, they knew she had been dead only a few days at most. The police also knew that the killer was picking up his victims with increasing frequency. They believed they would soon catch at least one of the three killers they thought were working the area. It was a race against time as they tried to piece together clues from interviews with Lake Avenue and Lyell Avenue prostitutes about the strange johns coming into the neighborhood.

"Who saw Trippi last?" they would ask. But the women could only stare blankly, because Shawcross had made it a point never to be seen with one of his victims. He picked them up on empty street corners and drove them to remote areas. He killed them quietly and drove their corpses to distant spots so he wouldn't be seen carrying them off or be spotted when he returned to cut out parts of their bodies.

The police were still interviewing women on Lake

Avenue late one December evening when prostitute Elizabeth Gibson saw Arthur Shawcross drive up in Clara Neal's Dodge. He stopped in front of a place he called Mark's Coffee Shop and got out to have a cup of coffee. Liz was cold. She'd been working the streets most of the day, staying out of the way of the police interrogation teams that were making like tough for all the women by driving away business. Johns don't like to solicit sex with vice detectives combing the neighborhood looking for an elusive killer and stopping every strange man looking out a car window. No, the legitimate johns were staying away and forcing the streetwalkers to become more aggressive in drumming up business. That was why Liz Gibson was so cold.

Liz knew Mitch's car. She'd seen it in the neighborhood. She'd even known a few girls who'd turned tricks with this guy—the "half-and-half" man—and laughed about the way he spent his money. He was okay, she thought, and climbed into the car to get warm. She'd only stay in there a few minutes. He wouldn't mind.

"Why are you in my car?" Art asked her when he came out of the restaurant a half hour later.

"I was cold," she said. "It's warm in here. I saw you drive up. You're Mitch. Can I stay in here for a few minutes?"

Shawcross drove her to a parking lot on the corner of Avenues D and St. Paul, where they stopped to talk.

"I don't want to screw," she told him. "But how much money do you have on you?"

"I got fourteen bucks," he said. "What can I get for that?"

"You can do oral on me," she told him.

Shawcross explained to the investigators that he gave her the money, which was all he had, and they stretched out across the front seat.

"I gave her oral sex," he said. "Then we lay together and I rubbed my penis against her. While I was doing this, she took my wallet out of my pants. I slapped her, took the wallet, and dropped it on the floor. Liz looked something like Mom. I slapped again and again."

Shawcross told the medical investigators that when he looked up at her after she had taken his wallet, the similarities between Liz Gibson and his mother, Bessie Shawcross, were so great that he kept on slapping her out of rage. He couldn't stop. Then Liz Gibson fought back and tried to get away. She kicked hard against him and then against the dashboard. Her foot broke the gearshift lever and bent it all the way over. Shawcross was seized by panic and rage.

"She grabbed onto my face with her fingernails that hurt and burned too," he told the investigators. "I pushed her away from me with my wrist. I kept pushing even after she relaxed."

As he described it to the police, Shawcross was pushing the meaty flat part of the side of his wrist across her throat to get her to relax her grip on his cheeks with her nails. He said that she was digging into his skin so hard and hurting him so much that his pushing her away was part of a reflex action. He kept pushing even after she relaxed, but he didn't remember how long he kept his wrist on her throat. Then he realized she had stopped breathing. She still reminded him of his mother. He began driving along the dark roads with the dead Liz Gibson stretched out across him in the front seat. He understood that he had become an

71

animal, he said, and it frightened him.

"I cried while I was driving. What was I becoming? I couldn't think right," he told medical investigators.

Shawcross drove his victim down County Line Road until he found a dirt turnoff and pulled into the woods. He took off all of Gibson's clothes and carried the body back into the woods, where he laid her out facedown. Then he returned to the car. He said that he was close to panic at this point and tried to return to his normal life as quickly as possible to quell the fears that were tossing about within his brain.

"I found three packages of cocaine in her coat. I tossed everything out of the car as I drove along. Then I went to the Dunkin' Donuts on Monroe Avenue and Alexander Street, had coffee and read the paper, then I went home. The next day I told Clara that I had an accident and broke the gearshift. She knew that I didn't do it, though. That was when she had doubts," he said.

Shawcross explained that by the time he had killed Liz Gibson, who was his ninth victim, the entire Rochester community was on fire over the stories of the serial killer roaming the red-light district. Although Clara Neal remained a steadfast friend to him, Shawcross said he nevertheless got the impression that she believed the stories he told her about going fishing and getting the newspapers on the very same nights the police were saying the victims had disappeared had made her suspicious. Now, he said, he brought the Dodge back to her with the broken shift lever and she realized that something was going on that he wasn't talking about. He himself was also acting strange, he said, because he felt that he was just on the verge of anger with every new girl who tried to solicit him. And the police were all over the place—on the streets, in the alleys, patrolling in their cars, and cruising past his favorite body dumpsites.

What Shawcross didn't realize was that the simple fact that he had returned to the June Stotts burial site to cut her body and take out her vagina had connected her murder to the Dotsie Blackburn murder and had established an M.O. for at least one of the serial killers the police were investigating. By having done that, Shawcross had given the police a reason to expect that the killer was returning to his victims to remove articles of clothing from them and cut out parts of their bodies. Moreover, because the police were finding fresh corpses, they had every reason to believe the killer was still in the area and would eventually be caught by high-intensity surveillance. It was a waiting game, and the area prostitutes whose lifestyles put them outside the law and at risk were the bait for the police trap, by default and not by actual design.

Less than two weeks after he dumped Liz Gibson's body in the woods, Shawcross told the police, he had parked Clara's Dodge in front of City Mattress on Lyell Avenue at about two in the morning and gone off to get himself some coffee. When he came back to the car, he saw a pretty girl with bright white boots leaning against the door on the passenger side of the car.

"She wanted fifty bucks," Shawcross told the police. But he said that he got her down to thirty. Then he drove her to the deserted parking lot of Westgate Plaza in an area where there was a row of five Salvation Army clothing dumpsters. There was a large Salvation Army trailer parked in the lot, Shawcross remembered, and he and his victim parked behind the trailer, well out of sight of Chili Avenue, which runs nearby. He said that he took off his clothing because the car was getting steamed up and he was very warm. She left on her white blouse and her stockings, but took off her skirt, her boots, and her underwear.

Shawcross said that he tried to have intercourse with her but could not get an erection. He couldn't even get his penis inside of her, he said. "She called me a wimp," Shawcross said. "She made fun of me." As he got angrier, he remembered, she began insulting him more and more. Finally he stopped.

"Faggot," the prostitute said. "You're no better than a faggot."

"I smacked her in the mouth," Shawcross told the police. And she said, 'I'm going to tell the cops. I think I know who you are, anyway.'"

But Shawcross had other plans.

"Well, you ain't going to tell nobody," he said, and grabbed her around the throat with both hands. He squeezed and squeezed her neck with his powerful hands until the woman became limp and slumped against the seat. Then he squeezed even tighter until she stopped breathing.

"She knew I was the killer of the other girls," he said to the police, who were interrogating him weeks after the murder of his tenth victim.

Shawcross said that he dumped her clothing in the Salvation Army box and then drove out of the area toward Buffalo. But on the way he made a wrong turn, he said, doubled back, and dumped the body into a heavy snowdrift covering a narrow creek alongside Redman Road, near Churchville. "I opened the car door and she went right over the guardrail," Shawcross told the police. "She rolled right over into the creek and landed on her back." In a later statement, Shawcross wrote that after he had rolled her out of the car and onto the frozen creek, "I kick snow on top of her to cover her up."

Shawcross told the police that he never returned to the spot where he'd dumped her—the victim's name was June Cicero—until the day he was arrested. He also told state police investigators that he didn't return to any of the bodies except June Stotts'. However, months later, Shawcross wrote a journal for the psychological investigators in which he said that two or three days after he had killed Cicero, he had bought a small single-bladed handsaw and returned to the frozen creek where he had dumped her body. "I went back to her. I had to pull hard to get her out of the ice. Also, I didn't park the car there, but up the road, near some houses, and walked down. I had the saw inside my coat. I went for the purpose of cutting out the sex organ and giving it to Clara's son Robert Lee. I did cut out her pussy and ate it raw, frozen. Dropped the saw in someone's garbage can."

Shawcross said that he had gone hunting with Robert Lee Neal on a number of occasions and "every time we got a deer, he kept asking for the sex organs of a female. All we got were males. Two of 'em." Shawcross said that he had been looking for animal sex organs to give to Bobby Neal, and might have thought at the time that he was going to give him June Cicero's. He wrote, however, that he was too excited about taking June Cicero's vagina for him to give it away. Therefore, he said, after he cut it out of her corpse with the single-bladed saw, "I pulled out the hairs and wrapped it in a bar towel. Went back to the car and came back to the city. Dropped the saw off at Wegman's dumpster on Chili Avenue. Drove down near Turning Point Park and sat playing with myself and that vagina. Then I put it in my mouth and ate it. I had no control at all."

Chapter 5
The Scene of the Crime

Shawcross didn't even remember the eleventh victim. He was so out of control after killing June Cicero that he only vaguely remembered picking up a black prostitute on Lake Avenue and letting her go. This was after he met Liz Gibson, who he dumped over in Wayne County, far from his normal burial sites, because he was afraid of being followed by the police. By January, Shawcross was haunted by the June Cicero killing and by the need to have sex with some of the corpses. He knew that the sites where bodies that had been discovered had already become crime scenes, but nobody had discovered June Cicero yet. Maybe he could still pull her out of the ice before the deep February freeze really set in.

One Wednesday morning, January 3, 1990, Arthur Shawcross decided to drive over to Salmon Creek in Northampton Park, where he had dumped June Cicero. It would be the second time he had visited her in the two weeks since he'd strangled her and thrown her body off the bridge. He'd been back once since then, when he'd cut out her vagina. Now maybe he'd have intercourse with her, he thought, or he'd just visit her like he'd visited with the corpse of eight-year-old Karen Ann Hill fifteen years earlier. Shawcross brought his lunch along, one of the packaged salads he prepared each morning at G & G.

Arthur told the police that he wasn't following the progress of the prostitute murders investigation in the newspapers or on TV. His wife Rose said that a few times, when news of the killings appeared on television, Shawcross would go into the other room and watch it, but didn't seem particularly disturbed about it. It was clear, though, that police surveillance in the area had increased. State and city police cars were crisscrossing through the red light district and waiting silently in the dark near the dumpsites where bodies had been found. They were trolling for the killer just as Shawcross had been trolling for victims. They were like darkened submarines running silently through the night.

Thus Shawcross kept to his routine during the days. He was wary of any marked vehicle until he drove by Salmon Creek on January 3 and saw no one there. He didn't notice that far in the distance, out of earshot, was state police helicopter 1H11, on surveillance patrol heading east across Salmon Creek. Shawcross pulled the car up to the top of the bridge and looked out across the frozen surface at the body of June Cicero encased in ice. He slid across to the passenger seat, opened the passenger door so he could see the body better, and began eating the olive salad he had brought with him from G & G Produce

78

that morning. That's when he heard the sound of rotors overhead and spun his head around in panic toward the helicopter swooping toward him.

New York State Police Senior Investigator John McCaffrey was riding in the helicopter along with Tom Jamieson and Technical Sergeants Kenneth Hunt and Mark Wadopian when he saw the shape of a body in the ice of Salmon Creek far in the distance as their aircraft hovered south of the Route 31 bridge. McCaffrey could see the white skin of the body just beneath the bridge, and the helicopter swept in for a closer look. The state police officers also saw a gray Chevrolet Celebrity parked on the southern lane of the bridge, about ten feet above the body. They saw a white man in the Chevy sitting on the passenger side of the front seat with the door opened. He told investigators later he'd been urinating in a plastic soda bottle. Aware of the chopper's presence as soon as he heard it swoop overhead, he closed the passenger door, slid across the front seat behind the wheel, and drove east on Route 31, away from Salmon Creek.

"Follow him, Mark," McCaffrey told Sergeant Wadopian, the chopper pilot, who hovered above the Celebrity as it drove along 31 to its intersection with Route 259, where it made a left and headed north into the town of Spencerport. "Stay on him. Let's get a ground unit on him."

The technical sergeant contacted State Police Trooper John Standing in unit 1E28 and asked him to drive toward Spencerport to pick up the Chevrolet. Meanwhile, Trooper Donald Vlack, in Unit 1E25 driving through Churchville, monitored the chopper's transmission and followed the Chevy into Spencerport. The troopers watched as the Chevrolet sped along 259 to where it became Union Street and to the intersection of West Avenue. The driver turned onto West and then onto Church Street. The car turned into a municipal parking lot across the street from the Wedgewood Adult Home and the driver parked, got out on the left side of the car, and walked into the home. He was a heavyset white male, the police wrote in their notes, wearing a beige jacket, bluejeans, and a baseball cap.

John McCaffrey directed Standing into the municipal parking lot, where the trooper pulled up behind the Chevy and waited. "That's it," McCaffrey told him as he stood behind the Celebrity in the parking lot. "That's the correct vehicle."

"The vehicle plate number is New York XLT-125," Standing radioed. And he saw Vlack's unit pull into the municipal parking lot. While Standing secured the Chevrolet Celebrity, Vlack entered the home and asked the people inside whether a white male had just walked through the doorway.

"He's down in the basement," someone said.

Vlack, along with a custodian and the director of the home, went into the basement, where they saw a white heavyset male matching the description McCaffrey had radioed from the helicopter.

"Excuse me, sir," Vlack asked the man. "Did you just come in from the outside?"

"Yes, Officer, I did," the man told him.

"May I see some identification, please?" Vlack

asked.

The man took out a New York State Department of Motor Vehicles nondriver photo ID. The name on the card was Shawcross, Arthur J., living at 241 Alexander Street, 101, Rochester, NY 14607. "What's the problem?" he asked.

"Were you driving that gray Chevrolet Celebrity in the parking lot across the street?" Vlack asked Shawcross.

"Yes, sir," Shawcross said. "I borrowed the car. I don't have a driver's license."

Vlack asked Shawcross for his phone number and went back to the parking lot with the information he had copied off Shawcross's photo ID. He radioed back to McCaffrey in the helicopter that they had a positive identification of the driver of the Celebrity which McCaffrey had seen leaving the scene of the unidentified body under the Route 31 bridge over Salmon Creek. Vlack and Standing then went back into the nursing home, where they found Shawcross sitting at a table in the basement.

"Are you the driver of the Chevrolet Celebrity in the parking lot?" Standing asked Shawcross.

"All this for taking a piss by the side of the road?" Shawcross asked him. He reached into a wastebasket by the card table and pulled out an empty Pepsi bottle. "You want this bottle?" Shawcross asked.

"Not right now, you can put it back," Standing said. "Would you mind taking a walk outside with us to answer a few questions?"

"Okay," Shawcross said, and picked up his jacket and baseball cap and walked outside, where Standing asked him if he would mind sitting in the back of the police car while they talked. "Sure," Shawcross answered, and climbed into the backseat.

John Standing, in front of Shawcross, picked up the microphone and radioed to the helicopter that the driver of the Chevrolet was sitting in the backseat of the police car. He turned to Shawcross.

"That your car?" he asked him, pointing to the Chevrolet.

"No, sir," Shawcross told him. "Borrowed it from a friend."

"Where'd you go with the car?" the trooper asked.

"I been to Brockport to pick up some lunch and was on my way back to Spencerport when I stopped by the park to take a piss," Shawcross said. "I threw the salad container into the creek and was gonna take my piss in the creek, too, but I saw the helicopter and took a piss in the bottle instead. I just drove on back to Spencerport." Then he laughed. "I guess I really opened up a can of worms when I took that piss."

"Mind if we go for a little drive?" Standing asked. "The other officer will watch your car while we're gone."

"Okay," Shawcross answered, and John Standing closed the rear door of the police car and drove a short distance to the Village Plaza. State Police Investigator Paul DeCillis pulled up in his car immediately behind them and spoke to Shawcross, who was still sitting in the rear seat.

"Would you please step outside, Mr. Shawcross?" DeCillis asked. He was respectful, deliberate, slow, but insistent. If he had his serial killer—if—he was not going to do anything that would skew his interrogation at the outset. Shawcross got out of Standing's unit and stood face-to-face with Paul DeCillis in the Village Plaza parking lot. "I'm Investigator Paul De-Cillis with the New York State Police," the detective said. "I'd like to ask you a few questions, just a few, and I wonder if you'd be more comfortable sitting in the front seat of my car while we talked."

Arthur Shawcross didn't answer right away. He nodded, walked to the passenger side of DeCillis's unmarked unit, opened the door, and sat down in the front seat. He watched while the investigator spoke with Trooper Donald Vlack, who had followed them to the Village Plaza in his unit, and then got into the front seat behind the steering wheel. He started up the engine and drove the car to a remote corner in the southern part of the parking lot where they were alone. He turned again to Shawcross, smiled at him, and said, "Let me tell you who I am again. I'm Investigator Paul DeCillis with the New York State Police. I would like to ask you a few questions. You are *not* under arrest. You are *not* in any trouble. If you don't want to answer any of my questions, you don't have to." DeCillis pulled an Admonition of Rights card out of his pocket. "You are not under arrest. You do not have to answer any of my questions at this time. You may have an attorney present when I ask you questions and when you give your answers. If you cannot afford to have an attorney present, an attorney will be provided for you at no charge. If you decide to answer questions, any answers you may give may be used against you in a court of law. Do you understand these rights as I have just read them to you?"

"Yes," Shawcross replied.

"Now that you have heard and understood your rights as I have read them to you, will you still talk to me and answer some questions for me?" the state police investigator asked.

"Yes."

"Please tell me what you were doing up on Route 31 earlier today when you were observed by our aerial unit," DeCillis asked.

"I was taking a piss," Shawcross said. "I had stopped over by the side of the road to take a piss in a bottle. When I saw the helicopter come over, I closed up and drove back to Spencerport."

"Who owns the Chevrolet Celebrity you were driving?" DeCillis asked.

"Clara Neal," Shawcross said. "I borrowed it from her early in the morning."

"Let's back up," the detective said. "Let's start early in the morning. When was the first time you saw Clara Neal in the morning when you borrowed the car?"

"I borrowed the car from Clara early this morning." Shawcross answered. "Very early. She has this bad back, you see. She got it a couple of months ago when she had an accident up on Route 31 near Sugar Creek. Since then it's been bad. I saw her this morning about twenty of four at her place on Morrill Street. I got to be at work, you see, from late at night to early in the morning, about three, over at the G & G Food Service on East Main in Rochester. I finished up and I went to Clara's right after work. She has to be at work at about six over at Wedgewood Nursing Home. She's a cook there. I got to her house and she was just getting ready to go. We stayed there until a quarter to six and then I drove her over to Wedgewood."

He paused to let DeCillis take all this in. It sounded plausible. It was even true, Shawcross said to himself, all of it. That's exactly what he'd done this morning. Then he continued.

"I dropped Clara off at work. You see, she can't drive because of her back, and I pulled the car over in the lot and went to sleep for a few hours. Woke up about ten and went for a drive over to Brockport for about twenty minutes. Just went driving. I was hungry and I brought an olive salad along with me that I made for myself at work this morning. So I ate it. Then I had to pee. So I pulled over to the side, slid myself across to the shotgun seat, opened the door on the right, and peed in this plastic soda bottle that I had in the car."

Then he demonstrated by putting his right leg out and showing how he could still sit in the car, open the door, and urinate into a bottle.

"Where'd you get the bottle?" the cop asked.

"Was already in the car when I stopped," he answered.

DeCillis was careful about his next question. The police already knew that at least one of the corpses in the serial murder investigation had been mutilated after death. Another corpse had a huge bite mark in the vaginal area. They didn't know when that had occurred, but they suspected the killer was returning to his dumpsites to have sex with and mutilate his victims. "You get outside the car for any reason?" he asked.

"No," Shawcross said. "I was in the car the whole time."

DeCillis thought for a second. He had to get to the details to see if he could trip the guy up or find any gaps in the story. It was sounding too good.

"You have a cap on the bottle?" he asked Shawcross.

"Yeah," Shawcross answered. "There was already a cap on the bottle. While I was peeing into the bottle, I heard this noise and turned around and saw this helicopter coming up behind me real low, so I put my thing back into my pants, put the cap on the bottle, got back behind the wheel, put on my seatbelt, and drove back to Spencerport."

"What did you do when you got back to the nursing home?" the detective asked.

"I gave Clara the bottle with pee in it and asked her to get rid of it. I said that a helicopter had followed me all the way into Spencerport after they saw me peeing in the bottle on the road. All of this because I was taking a pee in a bottle. That's all it was. So I told her to get rid of it," he answered.

DeCillis kept on probing, kept on pushing his questions into the fabric of his story, kept on trying to find the facts about Shawcross that would get him to come to his own admission about his relationship to the body frozen below the very spot where he had parked his car. The car, the body, the exposure of the man's penis: it was all too convenient to be a coincidence. DeCillis kept on pushing. He came around from a different side, knowing that Shawcross had built a defense for his actions that morning.

"Who's Clara Neal? Is she your wife?" he asked.

"Clara's a friend who works at the home from six to one P.M. We're not married to each other. I'm married to Rose," Shawcross said.

DeCillis saw at least one reason for the care Shawcross was taking with his story. The man was seeing someone on the side. Could there be more to this guy?

"Please tell me about your wife," the detective asked. "How old is she?"

"She was born, I think, on September 9, 1937," Shawcross answered.

"She live with you?" DeCillis asked.

"Yeah," Shawcross said. "She works right up here on the street," he continued, pointing up West Avenue to a cluster of small private houses.

"What does she do?" the police officer asked.

"She's a nurse's aide. She's working up here at 118 in a private house as a private nurse," Shawcross said. "She works out of the Visiting Nurse Service over in Rochester."

DeCillis asked Arthur Shawcross to show him the identification he'd showed to Trooper John Standing. He looked at the nondriver New York State DMV photo ID card and asked Shawcross whether he had ever had a driver's license.

"I had a license once," Shawcross said, "but I let it

expire back in 1970." And he handed him a New York State learner's permit that was issued a month earlier. "Clara's been teaching me to park so I can pass the road test again."

The year 1970—that was the police officer's clue. He knew he was getting warm. You always look for those gaps in a person's life. Many times they can mean only one thing. So he asked the next question very deliberately, but in his most unthreatening way. The answer had to come from Shawcross himself. "How come so much time's gone by since you let the license run out?" he asked.

"I been in jail," Shawcross told him.

"What for?" DeCillis asked.

"I got arrested back in 1972 for manslaughter," Shawcross said.

DeCillis went especially slowly now. Here he was, sitting directly across the front seat from a convicted killer who had just been spotted halfway out of his car right above one of the victims of a serial murderer and who was telling him that the only reason he was stopped at the dumpsite was to take a piss in a bottle. But this guy had been in the system. It was time to move it along.

"Where'd you do your time?" DeCillis asked.

"Downstate and Attica," Shawcross told him.

"I need to run a quick data check on the Chevy," DeCillis said to Shawcross as he called in the vehicle tag XLT-125. He got Clara's name back from the DMV along with her address and date of birth. Then he asked Arthur Shawcross about the salad he said he'd been eating while he was stopped above the body in the ice.

"Like I said," Shawcross told him, "I had made this olive salad at work and got hungry while I was driving around Brockport. So I stopped on the bridge and ate it and then threw the container into Salmon Creek. I took a pee after I finished. I never got out of the car or nothing. I seen the helicopter and drove away. That's when you guys came up."

"Okay, Mr. Shawcross," the detective said. "I just wanna talk to Miss Neal back there, and if you could wait for me here, I'd appreciate it. You want to cooperate with us to clear this up, right?"

"Yeah, yeah," Shawcross said as he saw Clara Neal walk up to the other state police unit parked behind them. It was just a little after one in the afternoon. It had been a long morning for Shawcross. It was going to get even longer.

DeCillis got out of the car to talk to Clara Neal. While Arthur watched them talk, presumably about the car and Shawcross's story of the events that had taken place that morning, another police officer walked up to DeCillis's police car and introduced himself to Shawcross.

"I'm Investigator Dennis Blythe," he said to Shawcross. "I just want to ask you a couple of questions, okay? First, you know why we're talking to you? What this is all about?"

"No, not really," Shawcross said. "Maybe because you guys caught me driving without a license?"

"You nervous?" Blythe asked him.

"Yeah, a little bit," Shawcross said.

"Well, you should relax," Blythe told him. "We'll

89

straighten everything out. I gotta get something to show you and I'll be right back. Wait here, okay?"

"Okay," Shawcross said.

Dennis Blythe returned almost instantly with a Voluntary Consent to Search form for Shawcross's apartment on Alexander Street. He brought another officer along with him. The detective was softspoken, almost friendly, as he explained what the problem was and why they needed Shawcross's help in getting to the bottom of some questions they had.

"You see, Art," Blythe said. "It seems the helicopter spotted you parked right above where they found a body recently. So there are a bunch of questions we need to have answered. It's all part of our investigation, and I'm sure that you're willing to help us in this investigation. Will you cooperate with us?"

"Sure."

"Okay. I have a Voluntary Consent to Search form here for your apartment. Would you mind if we went into your apartment to look around and, if we need to, to take some items back for us to look over?"

"I got no problem with that," Shawcross said.

Blythe handed the form to Shawcross to read and asked him to sign it at the bottom if he had no other problems with the form or the voluntary consent to search. Shawcross signed the form at 1:33, both Blythe and his partner Sergeant Brunett noted the time, and Blythe went back to his car. Arthur was alone. He looked over the controls in DeCillis's car. He looked back at Clara, who was still talking with the two state police officers in front of the uniformed trooper's black patrol unit. Blythe poked his head back into the front seat of DeCillis's car again.

Shawcross looked up, almost surprised to see him back so soon.

"I'd like to look inside the Chevy, if I can," Blythe said. "I know it's Clara's car and all, but since you were the last one driving it, we need to have your consent as well as hers. It's the way things are supposed to be."

Shawcross again told him he had no problem with their searching the car and handed Blythe his apartment keys. "The place is locked because no one's there," he told the investigator. "You need them to get in."

Blythe walked away and then came back with the consent forms. "I also need you to initial the changes I made about taking some of the items out of the apartment. We talked about that, just in case we need to take items back with us. Also for the car—if we need to hold on to the car or keep any items in the car. We need your consent to do that so I added it to these forms and need you to initial it, if you don't have a problem. Do you have a problem with that?"

"I don't have a problem," Shawcross told him.

Blythe showed him where he'd made the changes, Shawcross initialed the changes, and Blythe asked him if he'd mind going down to the Brockport State Police barracks for a while to answer some more questions.

"You know, there are a lot of people crowding around the parking lot and looking, and we'd like some privacy to talk about the investigation with you. We're not arresting you for anything, and you don't have to go anywhere you don't want to. But it would just get the answers out faster and clear up some of the questions we have."

"I don't have any problems," Shawcross repeated, and Blythe left him sitting alone in DeCillis's car while he went back to his own car. A few minutes later, DeCillis came back to the car and drove Shawcross out of the parking lot toward the Brockport barracks.

They drove along Main Street to Canal Road and then out of town to Route 19. Along the way, DeCillis kept repeating that he couldn't believe the nice weather they were having so early in January when it should have been much colder. He also asked Shawcross how he liked the area, especially the pretty houses along Gallup and Gordon Roads. Shawcross seemed polite enough, even though he was noncommittal. If he was feeling fearful in the police car, he didn't show it. He knew they wouldn't find anything in the apartment or in the car. He had taken great pains to dump everything. He also knew that there were no witnesses to any of his crimes. But he also wanted this to end. And he knew there would be some tough explanations ahead of him when the police got a hold of his prior arrest records. There would be many things to confront in the next few hours. Maybe it would be better to get it all out and go back on the inside.

Paul DeCillis brought Arthur Shawcross to an open area next to the main office of the state police barracks. When they got there, he asked him to wait while he got them some coffee.

"This won't take very long," he said. "We'll just wait for Dennis Blythe to get here and we'll all have a talk."

About a half hour later, Blythe walked over to Shawcross, who was still sitting in the reception area, and asked him to join him in his office.

"Do you mind doing this, Art?" he repeated. "You know, if you want to leave, you're free to leave right now, because we're not holding you for any crimes. You're not under arrest."

The two men walked to an office at the far end of the barracks where they sat down at one of the desks. Blythe pointed to a third man who walked into the room. "This is Charlie Militello, Art," Blythe said. "He's also a police investigator who wants to ask you a few questions so we can clear this up. Is that okay?"

"Sure," Shawcross said.

"Now, just what have you been told so far about all of this, Art?" Blythe asked.

"All I know is that there was someone's body found by the road where I was taking a piss in a bottle," he said. "That's all I know."

"So you're saying it was just a coincidence that you were in the area where the helicopter spotted the body, is that right?" Blythe asked him.

"Yeah," Shawcross said as Blythe turned the interrogation to a new tack.

"I need to know a little more about you, Art," Blythe began, "like whether you've ever been arrested before."

Shawcross knew he'd already told DeCillis that he'd been in jail on a manslaughter conviction, so Blythe's question didn't come as a surprise. Shawcross could only tell the truth. It was a truth the police already knew. "Yeah, I have," he said. As he expected, Blythe asked him about the circumstances of the arrest.

"There were these two kids that died," Shawcross said, trying to cut off any further discussion and leaving it up to Blythe to pursue.

"How old?" he asked almost before Shawcross could finish his answer.

"There was a boy who was ten and a girl who was eight," Shawcross replied.

"Were they your kids?" Blythe asked him.

"No!" Shawcross said firmly. Maybe he was trying to give the impression that he would never kill his own kids.

"Maybe you could give me some background about this," Blythe asked as he saw Shawcross fidget in his seat and hesitate, as if he were looking for just the right words. "I know it's tough, Art, but it's the past, and we have to have some information about you for the report and all."

"I knew the boy," Shawcross began, as if he were telling a long story. "I knew the boy's family. The boy used to come over to our place. I had to go out on this one day and the boy followed me. He kept following me and I told him to go home several times. You see, I was going to a party and the boy couldn't come with me, but he wouldn't go home when I told him to. He said, 'I'll go wherever I want

94

to,' and he kept on following me. That's when I hit him. Right here," he said, pointing to a spot right in the middle of his forehead between his eyes. "I hit him right here."

Blythe didn't wince. He didn't reveal any emotion other than concern for Shawcross, who was having a difficult time telling the story and who clearly was a very troubled person. But Blythe had to know. He had to know whether Shawcross killed with weapons or with his hands. The Genesee River Killer who might have murdered the woman whose body was right below Shawcross in Salmon Creek killed with his hands. Did Shawcross kill with his hands?

"How did you hit him, Art?" Blythe asked. "Did you use a weapon?"

Shawcross raised his wrecking ball of a right fist and pointed to it with his left hand. "I hit him with this," he said.

"How many times did you hit him?" Blythe continued.

"Just once," Shawcross said.

Dorothy Blackburn, the first victim they had found in Salmon Creek almost two years before, had had a huge bruise on her vagina as well as toothmarks around the wound where a piece of it was torn out of her. She had been strangled.

"What about the girl, Art?" Blythe asked. "How did you kill her?"

"I choked her," Shawcross said.

Again Blythe showed no reaction. He knew that he was dealing with a multiple homicide offender. The prostitute killer was a serial. Had Shawcross been a serial?

"Did you do both of them at the same time, Art?" he asked. "What was the time frame between them?"

"About three months," Shawcross said. "Killed the boy, then I killed the girl three months later."

"Can you tell me what the story was about the girl?" Blythe continued. A picture was emerging here that Blythe did not like at all.

"I was going through this thing about Vietnam," Shawcross told him. "You know, the war and flash-backs, and I had all these problems with my family, and there were other pressures, too. It was a spur-of-the-moment thing. I just grabbed her and choked her."

"How did it come to be that you and the girl were together?" Blythe asked.

"We were fishing," Shawcross answered. "And I just choked her, that's all."

"What I don't understand is why did you choke her when you were fishing?" Investigator Blythe said. "What happened when you were fishing with her that made you choke her?"

Shawcross paused for a while before answering. "You see, I seen psychiatrists. They didn't know why I choked the girl, and I don't know why I choked the girl. I still don't know why."

"Do you remember what the girl was wearing, Art?" Blythe asked.

"No, I don't," Shawcross said. "Shorts, maybe."

It seemed clear to the detectives from Shawcross's crimes and his time in psychiatric therapy—if Shawcross was telling them the truth—that he had at least been diagnosed as having sexual problems which led to violence. If the psychiatrists couldn't get an answer out of him, then he wasn't going to give them any cut-and-dried answers about his former crimes. Yet the man had a relationship with two women at the same time, one of whom was his wife. The other woman was giving him a car to drive around in. Both of these women were quite a bit older than Shawcross—they knew that from the DOB on Arthur's learner's permit and IDs and the DMV records of Rose Walley Shawcross and Clara Neal. Arthur Shawcross had been convicted of killing two small children fifteen years earlier. Maybe he was also seeing prostitutes, prostitutes in a wide enough age range to fit into a single victim profile. Time to bring the questions around to a new tack.

"Art, can you tell us a little bit about your relationship with Clara Neal?" Blythe asked. "I understand that you and Clara are lovers."

"Yes," Art told him, but did not elaborate.

Now Blythe started to turn up the heat about Shawcross's present circumstances.

"Do you think Rose knows about your relationship with Clara?" he asked.

"She probably does," Shawcross answered. "She's not stupid."

"Where do you work again?" Blythe quickly inserted to pick up the staccato pattern of questions and answers. He was adept at this, moving his subject along; he knew how to get things to the positive very quickly and then turn them back the other way. Maybe he'd get his confession out of Shawcross yet, if one was to be had.

"I work over at the G & G Food Service," Shawcross answered. "That's where I make up packaged salads for the day for schools and institutions."

"Let me back up and ask you where you were born," Blythe said, going for the easy answers to keep the dialogue going.

"Kittery, Maine," Shawcross said.

"And you lived there how long?"

"Not long at all, because we moved right away to Watertown."

"How long did you live in the Watertown area?"

"Until 1972," Shawcross answered, the date of his moving from Watertown coinciding exactly with his convictions for manslaughter. He hadn't moved of his own volition.

"You ever been arrested before?" Blythe asked him, building up the pattern of routine trust necessary to get Shawcross to rely on the investigator's authority. "Ever been arrested for anything else?" Blythe wanted him to admit to previous crimes. He wanted to get a pattern of confessions going. He did not want to be the man's enemy, only his confessor and confidant.

"Yeah," Shawcross answered. What the hell, it was all down in the record. The guy only had to check his rap sheet to find out everything he wanted Shawcross to tell him. "Been arrested for burglary and arson when I was 17 or 18."

"Could you tell me about it?" Blythe pursued.

"Broke into a store, that's all."

"When did you get out of prison?" Blythe asked.

Here was a man who had obviously spent more than a few years of his life in behind bars. How used to being on the outside was he?

"I got out in 1987."

"Where did you serve your time?"

"Green Haven."

"Where did you live after you got out of prison?" Blythe asked, now trying to get a pattern of the man's movements over the past few years. Why was he in Rochester, anyway?

"I went to the Volunteers of America in Binghamton, New York," Shawcross told him.

"That over on State Street?" Blythe asked quickly. He wanted a dialogue and wanted to verify as much of this as he could.

"Don't know. There was a big old church right by the river there. I had to go over a bridge above railroad tracks to get there."

"You mean you come up from downtown Binghamton on Chenango Street," Blythe said more than asked.

"Yeah, that's it."

"Was Taylor White across the street from you, Art?" Blythe asked.

"Don't remember."

"What about that low-income housing next to the church? Do you recall seeing that?" he asked.

"Nope, don't remember that either."

"Do you remember a big shopping center right nearby where you were staying? The Binghamton Plaza, it was called."

"Yeah, I remember a big shopping center right

99

near," Shawcross said, getting back into the pattern of agreeing with what Blythe was saying. Now it was time for straight questions and answers.

"How long did you stay at Volunteers of America?"

" 'Bout a month. Left in June '87."

"Who was the head person over there?"

"Some guy named Miller."

"What did you do there?"

"Cook."

"Who'd you work for?"

"Penny Thompson."

"Then where'd you go after you left Binghamton?" Blythe asked.

"Moved over to Delhi in June, 1987, to live with Rose Walley," Shawcross answered.

"Where'd you two live?"

"Downtown. Had a place there, but we had to leave after a week because the landlord screwed us. The landlord was under a lot of pressure to get rid of me," Shawcross revealed. He was getting a little hot under the collar about this, as if he'd really been wronged.

"Where'd you go next?" Blythe asked. Keep the questions moving about keeping Shawcross moving.

"Over to Fleishmanns."

"How'd you get there?"

"My parole officer, a guy named Zicarra, moved me over."

"Zicarra's first name was . . . ?" Blythe asked. Finally a name in the puzzle of Shawcross's past. He'd get some answers soon.

100

"Don't remember."

"How long did you stay in Fleishmanns?"

"Just a week, then we were out."

"Where to next?"

"We went to a hotel in Vestal, New York," Shawcross told him.

"Now, where was this hotel, Art?" Blythe asked.

"It was near the parkway. I remember it had a couple of big dogs and a swimming pool," Shawcross said, referring to the Vestal Parkway, which snakes out of the city and along the edge of the State University of New York campus. There is a long row of motels and hotels along the Vestal Parkway.

"Do you think it was closer to Binghamton or to Appalachin, New York?"

"No, it was further down from Binghamton. Closer to Appalachin."

"How come you left?" Blythe asked. He had already guessed the answer.

"There was a lot of publicity," Shawcross told him.

"And how long did you stay in Vestal?"

"One week, about."

"Where to next?" Blythe asked.

"Rochester."

A pause. Blythe let the silence hang.

"They sent us to Rochester," Shawcross said.

"And why Rochester?" Blythe asked, now more than a little annoyed that either nobody bothered to tell anybody at the city police or nobody at the city police bothered to tell the state police. He'd find out everything before this investigation was over.

"There was a lot of publicity in the other places, so they put us up in Rochester," Shawcross said. He spoke as if someone had once told him Rochester was a dumping ground for the human toxic waste of the prison system. Hey, disappear in Rochester; no publicity there.

"Where in Rochester?" Blythe asked.

"They put us up over on Lake Avenue, near an Amtrak station," Shawcross said as a small light of recognition went off in Blythe's brain. So Art knew the Lake Avenue neighborhood after all. Now to make some connections down the road.

"How long you live over on Lake Avenue, Art?" he asked.

" 'Bout two months."

"Where'd you move next?"

"Found a studio apartment at 241 Alexander Street. Apartment 107. Lived there with Rose, in the studio," Shawcross said.

And that brought him up to the present. Now it was time to get personal.

"Can you tell me a little bit about Rose Walley?" Blythe asked him. "Can you tell me what she's like? Tell me a little about Rose."

"She's nice," Shawcross said, either not knowing what to say next or not wanting to reveal anything about her he shouldn't.

"Well," Investigator Charlie Militello began, "can you describe her for us?"

"She's short," Art said, standing firmly on safe ground. "She's short, weighs about 170 pounds, and has dark gray hair."

"Know how old she is?" Charlie asked.

"Yeh, she's fifty-two."

"When was she born?"

"September ninth."

"Boy," Charlie Militello said as if in admiration, "you've got Clara and Rose. You're a good man."

"And you're how old?" Blythe asked him quickly, not giving him a chance to set up again from the previous compliment.

"Forty-four."

"What's your date of birth, Art?" Dennis Blythe asked.

"June 6, 1945."

"Who's older, Art, Clara, or Rose?" Militello asked.

"Rose."

"How is your relationship with Rose, Art?" Militello asked.

"Good."

"And," Militello continued, "how long have you and Rose been married?"

" 'Bout one year, but we lived together two years before," Shawcross answered.

"How'd you meet Rose?" Blythe said, picking up the back-and-forth from Militello as if the two had done this a hundred times before.

"When I was in Green Haven I was writing to her daughters and set up kind of a pen-pal thing with them," Art revealed.

"Now how did this get started in the first place?" Blythe asked.

"I was reading this wrestling magazine," Art said.

"Was looking at the ads in the back and found names of people you could write to who wanted to have pen-pals. They had an ad in there. I wrote to them and told them I was in prison and all. Then later on I got to know Rose through them. Wrote to Rose for ten years before I actually met her. After I'd been writing to them for ten years, they came to Green Haven to meet me in person. Then they came back on several occasions."

"Art," Charlie Militello broke in, "what are Rose's daughters' names?"

"Darlene Armstrong," Art began, but Blythe quickly cut him off.

"She lives where?"

"Near Walton, New York."

"That in a trailer?" Blythe asked.

"No, she got a house she lives in."

"Who does she live with, anybody?" Blythe asked.

"Yeah," Shawcross said. "She's married to Butch Barringer."

"Up in Walton?" Blythe asked again, keeping the discussion going, making conversation, making Shawcross feel comfortable talking about his family and his relationships, and, most important, building up the trust between what could be their serial killer and the investigators.

"Yeah."

"Up in a trailer near Loomis Brook Road?"

"I don't know."

"Art, how long was she with Butch?" Militello picked up.

"Can't say I know," Shawcross answered.

"I'm going to get myself some coffee, Art," Blythe said as he stood up. It was already after three and they'd been back-and-forthing with him for over a half hour. There'd be more to do throughout the afternoon, and they needed Shawcross with them in the questioning. "Can I get some for you? I'll make sure it's fresh."

"Yeah, that'd be good," Shawcross said, acting as if he and his investigators were already friends and there was nothing to be afraid of there. After all, they were just talking.

"You like to fish, Art?" Militello asked him.

"Yeah. Mostly for trout and salmon."

"You ever fish over in Lake Ontario?" Militello asked again.

"There and to the river."

"Where on the lake do you like to fish, Art?" Militello asked, trying to establish a pattern for Art's whereabouts at one of the areas where clues might have been left.

"Russell Station," Art said while Militello made a mental note of the name. They might well be conducting a search there in the next few days. "The water's warmer there because of the discharge from Rochester Gas & Electric."

Militello realized that Shawcross knew his fishing grounds and his local waters. If he knew where the water was warm, he'd know where people fished and didn't fish. He'd know where he could leave a body to decompose for weeks or months before anyone discovered it. And he'd know when hunting and fishing seasons opened and closed. He knew the area well.

"You ever work at Brognia Produce?" Militello asked.

"Yeah."

"Why'd you leave?"

"I just took another job at another place," Art told him.

"Let me get your coffee, Art," Militello broke in. "I think it's ready now." It was twenty after three when Charlie Militello reappeared in the office with Art's cup of coffee. Art liked to drink it black. "I want to say again, Art, that we really appreciate your cooperation in all of this. It'll clear up a lot."

Blythe came back into the office and without saying hello or anything asked Shawcross straight out if the parole board had moved him to Rochester. "Yeah," Art answered without even thinking about it.

"Now where did you work after you arrived here?" Militello asked him, picking up the pace of the interrogation again.

"All over the place 'cause Manpower sent me out on jobs."

"Who's your parole officer, Art?" Blythe asked.

Shawcross dug into his pocket and produced a business card. "Mahle," he said, and handed the card with Mahle's phone number over to the detectives.

"Tell us about what time Clara goes to work, Art," Militello said.

" 'Bout 5:45 A.M."

"And you?"

"I leave my apartment about 10:30 and work from

106

about 11 until I finish up."

"And when you're finished at work, Art," Militello continued, "where do you like to go?"

"Usually over to Jimmy the Greek's or over to Clara's or to the Dunkin' Donuts at Monroe and Alexander."

"How long have you been with Clara?"

" 'Bout a year."

"How'd it start, your relationship with Clara?" Militello asked him.

"I was chasing her daughter Loretta," Shawcross said. "I worked with her at Brognia's."

"Can you describe her?" Blythe asked.

"Sure. She was roly-poly and a lot of fun," he continued. "She invited me to a Christmas party at Clara's place, and that's where I got to meet Clara."

"Let's get back to today, Art," Blythe said. "Does Rose have a car?"

"No!"

"How does she get to work?" Militello asked.

"The Visiting Nurse Service sends a van to pick her up in the morning and drops her off at night."

"How often do you use Clara's car?" Blythe asked.

" 'Bout once a week."

"But," Blythe continued, "do you ever use it after you get out of work?"

"Only if I drive Clara to work and then go on errands for myself," Shawcross said. "Unless I do that, I don't use her car."

"That's how often?" Militello asked.

" 'Bout once a week, like I said," Shawcross repeated.

"And when you *do* use the car it's . . ." Militello began.

"It's when I come out after work."

"How do you and Clara drive around?" Militello asked. "You know, the two of you together. Does Rose know about it?"

"I don't know," Shawcross said.

"What time you get out of work today, Art?" Blythe asked him.

"Three A.M."

"What did you do when you got out?"

"Went to Clara's and slept on the couch until about 4:20," Shawcross said. "Then we left together at 5:15, I mean 5:45, and I drove Clara to work at the nursing home in Spencerport. Then, when I dropped her off, I parked across the street in the lot next to the dumpster and went to sleep. Woke up at 10:30 A.M. Then I took a ride to Brockport. Was sitting in the car in Ames Plaza over on Route 31 and ate my olive salad."

"Where in the plaza?"

"Right in front of the Village Donuts."

"Why? What were you doing there?"

"Lookin' at the pretty girls comin' out," Shawcross said as he smiled and shrugged his shoulders.

"Then what did you do when you left the plaza?" Militello asked him.

"Drove out of the plaza onto Route 19 for several miles."

"South?"

"Yes. I crossed over to Sweden-Walker Road to Route 31. I don't remember what road I took to get

108

over to Sweden-Walker."

"So did you go south," Militello asked, "to get to Route 31 where the helicopter spotted you? And what happened when you were on 31?"

"I went south to 31 but I had to pee very badly, so I got a bottle from the backseat of the car, slid over to the passenger's side, opened the passenger's door, swung over so my left foot was on the cement, and was peeing in the bottle when I heard the helicopter coming up. I got so scared I stopped peeing right away and put the cap on the bottle and left. Saw the helicopter following me in my mirror. I left the spot and went directly to where Clara worked. I found her in the kitchen area and asked her to come over. I told her what happened, about peeing in the bottle and being chased by a helicopter. I poured the pee out of the bottle and threw the thing in the trashcan next to the kitchen."

Militello and Blythe said nothing. They got up and walked to the door. "We'll be back in a minute," Blythe said, and they left him alone in the room, with the door wide open, where he sat for the next ten minutes.

Chapter 6
The Interrogation

"We want to ask you about the first two murders, Art," Blythe said to him when he came back into the room with Charlie Militello. "And I want to introduce you to Tony Campione, who's a state police investigator also." Shawcross and Campione shook hands. "You know, Art," Blythe continued, "you can leave any time you want to, but we would like to talk to you further about this so we can clear it up."

"No, it's okay," Art said.

"Good, 'cause we'd like to go back a little bit and talk about your problem in Watertown. Now we know that's hard for you and appreciate the way you're cooperating with us," Blythe began "Do you remember the name of that little boy in Watertown?"

"Jack, I think."

"Can you describe what happened? You know, *how*, the circumstances, as best you can," Blythe said.

"I was going to a party where my wife was. On

110

the way to the party the boy was following me for over an hour. It was getting me mad. I told the boy he had to go back home."

"And . . ."

"Finally I just turned around and hit the boy."

"How?"

"I hit him just once with my fist in his head and he fell right down. I just turned around and left. Left him there."

"Where did this happen, Art?" Blythe asked him as the tension and the pressure in the room increased. Here was a guy confessing all over again to the child murders that had driven him out of community after community downstate until the parole board had dumped him in Rochester. These were buried memories, Blythe knew, but if he could get him into the habit of confessing, maybe he'd confess to the prostitute murders. At least, that was the plan. It would all be in the confession, because they had nothing else. "Do you remember where this happened? Where you killed the little boy? Can you describe the place?"

"In a field with some woods in it. I guess you'd call it semiwooded. There was a swamp area there with a couple of inches of water. That's where I left the boy, in the swamp."

"This have anything to do with sex, Art?" Blythe asked.

"No."

"You ever have sex with the boy?" he asked again.

"No."

"Did you know the boy? Did you have any contact with the boy?"

"I used to go fishing with him," Shawcross said. "I knew him. Then after I left him in the swamp, about a day later, the boy's mother came over and asked me if I had seen the boy. I said no. Can't even remember how much time passed before they found him in the swamp."

It was clear that this was not a "stranger murder." Shawcross knew the victim. He probably knew him more intimately than he was willing to admit to the cops in the interrogation room. Did he know the little girl, too? Is that how he was able to get as close to her as he did? Was this the same pattern as the prostitute murders?

"What about the little girl, Art?" Blythe asked. "What was her name?"

Shawcross paused for a long time before he shook his head and told them that he couldn't think of her name. Maybe he could describe her.

"Can you tell us what she looked like? As best you can," Blythe pursued.

"Yeah. She had either blond or brown hair—maybe light brown—down to her shoulders."

"She developed? She have any boobs yet?" Blythe asked.

"I don't remember. I think she had kind of an average build," Shawcross said, specifically not picking up on what most pedophiles might look for in a young girl.

"Was she pretty?"

"Yes."

"Where'd this happen?" Blythe asked. "Can you describe the area at all?"

"I'd been fishing around Mill Street in Watertown for a couple of hours. It was right where the water comes off the Black River."

"Was the little girl with anybody else?" Militello asked.

"No, she was alone," Art said. "That's what I asked her, 'How come you're down by the riverbank alone?' She said that she always liked to come down to the river."

"What was she wearing?"

"Shorts, I think. Or pants."

"How long were you with the girl?"

"Only about ten or fifteen minutes."

"You have sex with the girl?" Blythe asked matter-of-factly and without pausing.

Shawcross only nodded and said yes very slowly.

"Was the girl alive when you had sex?" Blythe asked.

"Yes, she was."

"Did she take her clothes off, Art?" Blythe continued, trying to look for a pattern. Some of the dead prostitutes were still dressed. Some of them were naked. That was part of the puzzle of the case.

"I didn't take her clothes off," Art said. It was a curious answer because Blythe didn't ask him if *he* took her clothes off, only whether the girl took her

113

own clothes off. Whose clothes did Shawcross take off? The prostitutes'? This was an important statement.

"Did you take your clothes off, Art?" Blythe asked, not giving anybody time to think about anything.

"No. I had my pants down."

"What did you make the girl do?" Blythe asked. "Was she standing up? Was she lying down?"

"She was bent over."

"Pants down?"

"Yes."

"So you went in from behind?" Blythe asked. He could see the scene for himself, but he had to retain his composure.

"Yes. I think I put my dick in her."

"This is real tough for you, Art," Militello said. "We know that. We know you're doing real good. Real good. We appreciate your help in this."

Just when Shawcross should have begun to falter, Militello's praise and encouragement kept him going. It was the way it was done. As hard as the confessions get, you have to be on the suspect's side. He's helping you. You're helping him. You're partners in solving the same crimes.

"You know sometimes I try to forget the past," Shawcross said.

"I know, Art," Militello said. "That's why we know this is tough."

"Were you still having sex with her when you choked her?" Blythe asked.

"She was standing up when I choked her," Shawcross answered, indicating that the sex was over.

"You think maybe she wanted to have sex with you and that's why she came down?" Blythe asked, maybe to give him a motive for having sex. After all, the prostitutes wanted to have sex with their killer also.

"No. I don't think she wanted to have sex with me at all," Shawcross said. "She was standing there crying and bleeding."

"Wow, this really has got to be tough for you to talk about, Art," Militello chimed in again. "That's why we really appreciate it."

"Then what happened?" Blythe asked.

"Then . . . I don't know," Shawcross said. "But I think I killed her."

"Did she lead you on or anything?" Blythe asked. Maybe Shawcross saw all girls as leading him on, especially the prostitutes.

"I had this thing with my youngest sister," Shawcross suddenly said from very far away. "She was three years younger than me. I told my mother."

"What? What did you tell her?" Blythe asked. They had opened up a vein here.

"I said that we were more than brother and sister."

"Where does she live now, Art?" Blythe asked. "Your sister."

"Dexter."

115

"What's her name?"

"Jeannie Williams. She used to be married to a trooper and they lived in Greece."

"What were you and your sister doing?" Blythe asked him.

"Was this a kind of touchy-feely thing, Art?" Militello asked. "Or was it intercourse?"

"Wasn't intercourse," Art said.

"Then it was what?" Blythe asked.

"I ate her," Shawcross said. "I touched her."

"How long did this go on, Art?" Blythe asked him. "How old was your sister when this started?"

"She was a teenager," Shawcross said. He hesitated once or twice, as if it was painful for him to describe it. "Maybe 14 or 15. And it went on for three years. Maybe until she was 17."

Without a pause, Blythe asked again, "What did you do after you choked the little girl?"

"Nothin'. I don't remember. I just went home and left her there. Later the police came."

"I know how tough this has been for you, Art," Militello repeated. "But you have to know how much we appreciate your being so honest with us."

The three investigators then brought the questioning back to Shawcross's arrival in Rochester, going over information he'd already given them, checking the facts for discrepancies in the story, checking employment information, and trying to establish a pattern for Shawcross's movements in Rochester over the previous two years. Who did Shawcross know in the area? Were there any people who'd seen him with prostitutes? Did he have any fishing buddies? Where did he like to fish? Did his fishing spots put him where some of the bodies were dumped? Might he even remember if he dumped any of the bodies since he had admitted that he liked to forget what were unpleasant feelings? When they got Shawcross to admit that he liked to fish in Driving Park, they were able to put him at another one of the body dumpsites. He had been spotted at Salmon Creek, and now he admitted to fishing at Driving Park.

Now Tony Campione wanted to develop more information about where Shawcross fished and who might have seen him at various locations. They wanted him to open up, reveal specific facts about himself that they could later check up on with the prostitutes in the area who might have seen him. "So you been anywhere else besides the river and Driving Park?" Campione asked.

"Been over to Cliffside," Shawcross said. "Fell down the bank about eighty feet and broke my foot."

"When was this?" Campione asked, remembering that one of the prostitutes talked about a guy who had once limped.

"Last June or July," Shawcross said. "Went to Genesee Hospital where some Dr. Wenner gave me a cast that you strap on."

"Must have been tough to fish with that thing on," Campione said.

"Nah, went back to fishing the next day, but it

117

made me limp," Shawcross said.

Next, the detectives worked on his relationship with the Neals, his affair with Clara, and his friendship with her son Donnie, who was doing construction work over at the Roxbury Inn in Brockport. Then they brought the questioning over to Shawcross's job at G & G: "What time do you get there?" "What kind of salads does G & G make and sell?" "Who buys 'em?" "What do you do there?" "What's your typical day like?" "What do you put in the salads?" "What goes into an olive salad, anyway?"

"You put any ceci beans or garbanzo beans in that olive salad, Art?" Charlie Militello asked him.

"Nah," he answered. "They don't put those beans in an olive salad."

"Now let's talk about Clara Neal's daughter, Art," Blythe asked him. "What's her name again?"

"Loretta."

"Tell us about her. Where's she living? How'd you meet her?"

"Lives over in West Virginia, now," Shawcross began. "Clay County, where she's living with her four brothers and her father. She's kind of heavy-set, and now she's pregnant. She used to chase everyone around the warehouse but me. She thought I was a father figure."

"You ever have sex with Loretta?" Blythe asked him.

"Just a little grab-ass," he said, "but no intercourse. She was just a bitch. She'd run around the

118

warehouse with everyone but me."

"I want to ask you more about Clara," Blythe continued. "When you saw her, what you did, where'd you go?"

Shawcross told them that he saw Clara very frequently. "We'd just drive around," he said. "Sometimes out to Route 104, sometimes we'd go out to the parking lot near the Salvation Army boxes, and sometimes we'd go out to Waterport, where Clara's older brother lives."

"You have sex with Clara?" Blythe asked.

"Yes," he said. "About once every two weeks. I also seen a psychologist twice because I have a problem with sex."

Blythe asked him what the problem was.

"I can't keep an erection, you see. Can't have an orgasm. Maybe it's because of guilt from my past."

Blythe began asking him to elaborate, but Shawcross told him that it really wasn't his idea about the guilt. The psychologist had told him that guilt might keep him from having an orgasm.

"Well, how is sex with Clara?" Blythe asked, now as curious about the answer as he was interested in moving Shawcross toward a confession if Shawcross was the serial killer they were looking for.

"I can keep my erection longer with Clara than with Rose," Shawcross said. "She blows in my ear and puts her tongue in my ear. That helps me stay erect longer with her than with Rose, but I still can't have an orgasm."

He said that his relationship with his wife Rose

was good, that he liked her, but that he still had problems in bed. "When I have sex with Rose, she gets on top, and that way I can keep my erection."

Blythe asked him about adult movies and dirty magazines — pointed questions for anyone implicated in sex murders — but Shawcross said that nothing helped him at all. "I can't come because it hurts me physically," he revealed. "That's even why I can't keep up my erection."

"You seen a doctor about this?" Militello asked. "Did you have a physical exam recently?"

"Yeah, everything was okay."

"Does being with a strange woman help you get an erection?" Militello asked, homing in one critical issue of the interrogation.

Shawcross hesitated for a long time, as if he were processing information before answering. But Blythe jumped right in, throwing him off balance. "You know, like hookers," he said.

"I never had sex with a hooker," Shawcross said. "Because I didn't want to catch AIDS."

"But besides Rose and Clara, who else did you have sex with?" Tony Campione asked Shawcross.

"Dorothy Walker," Shawcross told them.

"Who is she and where does she live?" Blythe asked.

"She's about 42 and lives over on South Avenue." Shawcross answered. "She's white, got long black hair past her shoulders, cute-looking, sort of thin, and has cupcake boobs. I had sex with her once, but couldn't come."

They talked some more about Art's relationship with Clara, where he liked to hunt, and where he took her to have sex. They talked about Donnie Neal, about his pickup truck, and about how he and Art would sometimes hunt deer together. Then Tony Campione asked Art about Clara Neal's other car, the light blue-gray Dodge that had been seen frequently in the Lake Avenue district. Maybe there were clues in that Dodge, the police thought, that might give them some concrete evidence that would put Shawcross at the scenes of the crimes.

"What happened to that Omni that Clara and you were driving?" Campione asked Shawcross.

"It got hit near Ogden and it's over in a garage there now, near Trimmer, up by Parma Motors." And Campione made a note of that right away. That car would later turn out to be one of key pieces of evidence the police would ever have against the invisible killer who'd been able to move about the area for two years without being seen until just that morning.

As the police regrouped for another round of questioning and softening up a guy who was looking more and more like their suspect, they asked him if he would come along with them for some dinner, their treat. Shawcross again said that he had no problem helping out their investigation.

"But first we need some pictures, Art," Blythe said. "Do you mind? Just some photos."

"What for?" he asked.

"Just to move the investigation along. You know,

121

you've been so cooperative all this while, I'm sure you want to continue to cooperate."

Shawcross simply nodded and said they could take all the pictures they wanted. By about five-thirty on the afternoon of January 3, the police had their photographs and were on their way in Charlie Militello's car to the Pantry Restaurant, where Arthur Shawcross filled up on slices of Dutch apple pie and coffee.

"You hunt, Art?" Tony Campioine asked Shawcross at the restaurant. "I hunt."

"What do you hunt?" Shawcross asked him, trying to make conversation.

"Deer," the police officer said.

"You ever hunt deer with a knife?" Shawcross asked.

This was exactly what Campione was looking for, the details of the man's life of killing, the weapons he used, and the way he saw objects that he was about to kill.

"C'mon, get out of here," Campione said. "You can't hunt deer with a knife!"

"Sure can," Art said, almost proud of the way he was going to describe it. "You get yourself some farm salt and you crush it and set up in a container right on the ground in an orchard near water. Then you put the powder from shotgun shells in another container by the salt."

"You mean black powder?" Militello asked.

"Yeah. Then you find a tree and you climb it so you can see the salt and powder and then just wait. You see, deer are attracted to the salt by the smell. They come right up and lick it, lick the gunpowder, drink water, and then go back to the salt. They do this a few times and they can't move no more. Then you can climb down from the tree and cut their throats with the knife."

"How come the deer stand still?" Militello asked.

"The black powder acts like a tranquilizer. The deer know they're in danger, but they can't move well."

"You get right out of here, Art," Campione said." You're kidding us!"

Art started laughing. "No, no," he said. "I'm not kidding at all. You can also do something similar with eels. You see, after you catch an eel, they squirm around and are tough to get off the hook. By putting the butt of a cigarette down its throat, the nicotine causes them to stiffen. See, that's how you can get the hook out."

"So you were in 'Nam, Art?" Militello asked, picking up the conversation and turning it toward more of Shawcross's killing experiences. From killing animals in the woods to killing Vietcong in the jungle to killing prostitutes by the Genesee River, it might all be the same to Shawcross. They would soon find out.

"Spent thirteen months over there as a weapons specialist at Pleiku, Da Nang, Hue, and other places, moving ammo to different firebases in the hills," Shawcross said, but didn't elaborate.

"And in Green Haven, Art? What'd you do

there?" Militello asked again.

"Took me a correspondence course to be a lock-smith." Shawcross said. "You see, Master Locks have several master combinations for all their locks. However, there is one single combination that opens all Master Locks." He was expounding now. "But for any other combination lock other than a Master Lock, you can take a shoestring, wind it around the dial, then pull it and spin it like a top, and the lock will open."

"But why, Art," Campione asked, "didn't you just become a locksmith when you got out?" If the guy really knew as much as he said he knew, he should be making money and working instead of fishing off a pier and becoming a suspect in the area's worst serial murder case in history.

"Cost me $25,000 to get bonded as a locksmith to get a job," Shawcross said. "I didn't have that kind of money, especially being in jail. They should've said something about that in the corre-spondence course I took."

When they brought Arthur Shawcross back to the Brockport station, they all realized they were finished for the night. There was nothing more they could ask him. They wanted to check on his facts and circulate his photo around to some of the hookers on Lake Avenue who might have seen him with some of the victims, and they wanted to lo-cate the Dodge Omni to see whether any clues had been left inside. The Dodge that had been spotted in the Lake Avenue district had been sitting in the garage for weeks, waiting for someone to look inside for clues.

"We're going to get you home now, Art," they said.

"What about Clara?" Shawcross asked. "She got no car now?"

"Donnie Neal's at the station," Blythe told him. "He'll take his mother home." And Investigators Dennis Blythe, Charlie Militello, and Tony Campione piled Shawcross back into the car for the drive back to Alexander Street in Rochester.

"You know, Art," Blythe said to him as they approached the apartment building, "we may want to talk to you tomorrow about some of the things you told us today. Do you think you'll have any problem with that?"

"No, I won't."

"Then let me give you my business card, also with my phone number on it, just in case you have anything you remember that you want to tell me about," Blythe continued.

As they dropped him off in front of the house after the twenty or so minute drive, Blythe reminded him of his promise to talk to them on the next day if they wanted him to. "In fact," Blythe said, "maybe we really will stop by tomorrow to talk to you a little bit."

"Okay," Shawcross said as he shook hands with the three detectives.

Shawcross was visited later that night by two more officers who returned his keys. After that, he went to bed, sniffling off the effects of a cold he was trying to get over, and not realizing that he was already at the very center of one of the most intense multiagency investigations ever conducted in Rochester. Detectives from the state police and the city police were now comparing notes, checking witnesses, impounding the Dodge, taking tire impressions, fact-checking Shawcross's story, and assembling his case file from state prison records. Whatever was going on in Arthur Shawcross's mind as he went to bed on the night of January 3, 1990, we may never know. Whether he was fearful or confident, we may never know. Whether he realized that his apartment had been completely staked out by surveillance teams from the state and city police, we may never know. But by the time Shawcross walked out of his apartment the next morning, the trap the police had set for him was just about to snap shut.

Chapter 7
The Confession

Dennis Blythe was sitting in his unmarked surveillance unit listening to his police radio softly crackling away while he watched Arthur Shawcross limp down the short flight of stairs at 125 St. Paul Street in Rochester and unlock his bicycle from a bike rack in front of the building. It was January 4, the morning after Shawcross had been spotted by the state police helicopter making a routine pass over Salmon Creek. Without a word, Blythe turned to his partner, Investigator Leonard Borriello, and motioned for them to intercept Shawcross before he rode his bike away. The two slid out of the car and were across the street before the chubby 44-year-old Shawcross had a chance to mount his bike.

"Art," Blythe said as he walked up and shook his hand, "this is Investigator Lenny Borriello. I want you to meet him."

Borriello stuck out his hand, Shawcross took it, and Borriello said, "thanks for cooperating with Investigators Blythe and Militello yesterday, you were really a help. Yesterday you said that we could talk to you again today if we needed to. Is that still okay?"

Shawcross nodded.

"Would you be willing to take another ride with us to Brockport to talk some more?" Borriello asked.

"Sure," Shawcross said. Shawcross locked his bike back up to the rack while the cops stood there looking at him and then walked with them to the police unit across the street. He got in the right rear door while Blythe slid along side him in the rear seat and Borriello got behind the wheel.

"First off," Blythe began, "I just want to ask you about some things that didn't match up in your story yesterday. Inconsistencies. But before going on, I just want to advise you again of your rights again right here. Art, you do not *have* to talk to us or make any statement at all." Blythe pulled out a "five-warning" notification and waiver sheet and read from it. "You have the right to remain silent—you do not have to say anything if you don't want to. That anything you say can be used against you in a court of law. You have the right to talk to a lawyer before answering any questions and to have him here with you. If you cannot pay for a lawyer, one will be given to you before any questioning, if you wish. If you do wish to talk with me, you can stop at

128

any time. Art, do you understand what I have just said to you?"

"Yes."

"Do you agree to give up your rights and talk with me now?"

"Yes."

"Thanks, Art," Blythe said, jotting down the time at 11:45 A.M. as he initialed the notification and waiver card and wrote the word "yes" twice to Shawcross's acknowledgment and subsequent waiver of his rights. "I really appreciate your co-operation. Before we go down to Brockport I want to drive over to Durand Eastman Park. That may refresh your memory of an encounter with a prostitute."

About a half hour later, the two detectives and Shawcross had parked on a road leading to the golf course at Durand Eastman, and Borriello asked Shawcross if being at the park prompted him to remember an incident with a prostitute on the day before the previous Thanksgiving at about four in the afternoon.

"Yes," Shawcross said. "There was one right about that time, but I can't be sure of the exact date."

"Yeah, well, that was one of the inconsistencies we wanted to talk about," Blythe said. "Let's get down to the station and talk this over a little more."

While they headed over to the Rochester Public

Safety Building, Leonard Borriello told Shawcross that he had gotten some information from a prostitute named Jeanne VanNostrand that he wanted to talk to him about. "You see, she told me that she was with you on the day before Thanksgiving in the park and that you told her you worked at G & G and that you had a plastic brace on your injured leg. She said she had this knife and she pressed it against your leg when you were having sex. She said that you had taken her to Durand Eastman Park, where you parked on the road leading up the golf course, and that you had a blue car at the time. She said you had a rifle scope between the seats and that you gave her potatoes and apples in plastic bags which you had taken from farmers. That's what she said, Art," Borriello explained.

Shawcross didn't say anything.

"Then she said that a few days after Thanksgiving she saw you and a woman passenger in the Omni at a little after two in the morning going across the Bausch Street Bridge and heading north on St. Paul Boulevard. The girl's name in the car with you, by the way, was Elizabeth Gibson. She was wearing a pink coat, Jeanne VanNostrand said. Art? What do you think?" Borriello asked.

"I don't remember the name VanNostrand, but I was with a prostitute in Durand Eastman Park, and I remember telling her that I worked over to

G & G," Shawcross said.

As Borriello drove the car over the Bausch Street Bridge on his way back to the Rochester Public Safety Building, he asked Shawcross, "You remember picking up a girl here?"

"Yeah," Shawcross replied from the backseat. "But over on the west side of the bridge, not the east." And they drove the rest of the way to the Public Safety Building, where they arrived at about 12:40 and set up in the conference room along with investigators Tony Campione and Charlie Militello. Later on, they would be joined by Investigator William J. Barnes, who would complete the interrogation team.

"I want to remind you of your constitutional rights again, Art," Dennis Blythe began. "You know that you don't have to talk to us if you don't want to and that you can have a lawyer in here if you want one before we ask you any questions. Do you have any problem talking to the police about any of this, Art?" Blythe asked.

"No. I got no problem," Shawcross said. "I'll speak to the police."

Leonard Borriello turned over a photo of Elizabeth Gibson and waited while he looked at it. "Art, why is it that you were seen with this woman eleven hours before her body was discovered over in Wayne County?" he asked.

There was no answer.

"You should also know," he continued, "that

we found a paint chip near her body that can be matched to the blue paint from the car you were driving, at the time." He waited. "There are also tire impressions that can be matched up."

"Well," Shawcross said, "a paint chip can come from anywhere and I don't even know that you got a paint chip."

"Art, who drives that car besides you?" Blythe asked him. "Think about that. We all know the car belongs to Clara and we'd hate to think that Clara was involved. Tell me, specifically, was Clara involved?"

"No. Clara was not involved in this," Shawcross said. "I was involved in this."

Blythe brought a typewriter back into the conference room so that he could take Shawcross' full statement and have him initial it. He read out Shawcross' full Miranda warnings and asked Shawcross to read them and initial them. At that point, Shawcross made his statement to Dennis Blythe, Leonard Borriello, Charlie Militello, Tony Campione, and Bill Barnes.

"Sometime after November 24, 1989," he began, "I was driving Clara Neal's Dodge Omni in the City of Rochester. I was sitting at Mark's Restaurant on Lake Avenue where I had just had a cup of coffee. I was sitting in my car in the parking lot when a female who was white said her name was Theresa came over to me and started talking. I had seen and talked to her before, but I had never gone out with her before. She asked me if we could go for a ride. I said yes. I said, 'Where to?' She said 'Go across the bridge,' which is toward Upper Falls Boulevard. She then said to make a left on St. Paul. This was going north. She then said, 'Just drive.' We made a turn and got onto Route 104. We were going east. Then we got down on County Line Road. I don't know the name of the town it's in. I know now that it's in Wayne County. We were talking about all sorts of things: sex, drugs, her life. Just general conversation. She told me that she lived on the west side of town. She told me she was trying to get off of drugs. She didn't tell what kind of drugs. She asked me what I preferred, meaning sex. I asked her how much she wanted. She told me we would talk about that later. I told her that it was hard for me to get a hard on. She told me she could fix that. We made a right turn down a dirt path. She told me to back down in. We were about twenty yards down this road. Not very far. I didn't want to get stuck. We then started talking about my sex problem, and she said she could take care of that. She pulled her pants off and put them on the floor in the front. The coat she laid over the seat. She had all of her clothes off. I unbuttoned and unzipped my pants. She started giving me oral sex. I was playing with her pussy. I moved a little bit and then I noticed that my wallet was out of my

133

pants. I told her to hold it a minute. I put my
wallet in my front pocket. She then asked me to
take my pants off. She wanted to play with my
balls. I had a semi-erection so I took off my
pants and I mounted her. Then she just grabbed
me with both of her hands and dug into my face
and eyes. I was rearing back and asked her,
'What are you doing?' She didn't say nothing. She
just kept holding on. I tried to push her away
from me with both of my hands and forearm.
My arm had gotten underneath her chin. I just
kept on pushing and she started getting weaker
until she stopped altogether. She let go. I might
have panicked and just kept on pushing. I don't
know. Then I tried to revive her. I shook her and
tried to give her mouth-to-mouth, but nothing
happened. I got out of the car and picked her
up. I was crying. I didn't know what to do so I
carried her back down the path. I don't know
how far I carried her, but it was quite a ways. I
seen a dark shadow that looked like an old farm
tractor and I carried her past the tractor into a
field. I laid her down and I turned around and
went back to the car. I sat in the car and got the
rest of my clothes on and started driving aim-
lessly. I came down through the Lake Road past
the nuclear plant and I think I turned down the
hard Road or the Salt Road. I knew that I would
eventually get back to Route 104. I started coming back on 104 when I saw her clothes on the

floor, so I cranked the window down and threw the clothes out the window. When I got as far as the Irondequoit Bay Bridge, I pulled over by the guardrails. This was on the west side of the shoreline, but the north side of the bridge. I got out of the car, crying, thinking about what happened, and then I opened the car door. The light came on and I saw her pink coat still in the car. I took it out and threw it over the bridge. I don't know if it landed in the water or not. It's possible that it landed in the brush under the bridge. I then drove home on Alexander Street. I kept Clara's car overnight."

Shawcross indicated in his statement that he was looking at a photograph of Elizabeth Gibson and this was indeed the woman he had killed and the one whose death he had described to the police. Shawcross also said that while he was driving Liz Gibson out of Rochester he passed a woman standing on the corner of St. Paul Boulevard. This, the police assumed, was the woman Jeanne VanNostrand who said she had been with Shawcross at Durand Eastman Park on the day before Thanksgiving. She was the woman who put Shawcross and Gibson together on the night of the murder.

"I feel bad that this happened," Shawcross told the police investigators in the room. "I'm sorry that it happened." And he signed his statement and allowed Dennis Blythe and Leonard Borriello to witness it for him.

The police had gotten their serial killer and had his confession to at least one of his crimes. They knew the cases could be cleared. Now they had to go for as many as they could get.

"Is there anything else I can get you, Art?" Blythe asked him.

"All I want is my wife brought in," Shawcross said.

"I'll make the arrangements for that," Blythe said, and left the conference room where Shawcross was sitting reading over his statement.

Len Borriello sat across from him, simply watching the confessed killer look at the paper in his hands as if it were his only future. He watched the man for about ten minutes. Then he looked up at the doorway and was motioned by another officer to step outside.

"We found an earring inside the rented car," he was told. "It matches the one found on the body of June Cicero."

Borriello waited in the doorway for Blythe to return, keeping an eye on Shawcross. Then they both sat down with Shawcross just as he finished reading his confession to the Gibson murder that Blythe had typed up.

"Is it okay?" Blythe asked him.

"Yeah, it's okay," Shawcross said.

"Then can you sign the second page for me and initial the first?" Blythe asked.

After Art put his initials on the page, Borriello told him about the earring. "The earring on your seat was the same earring that they found in the body of the woman who was in the creek where you parked yesterday, Art," Borriello said.

"Well, how do I know you even have an earring? Besides, it could be anybody's earring. How do I know?" Art asked, now digging in after the first confession.

Blythe and Borriello looked at each other, got up, and left the conference room, and another team, Investigators Barnes and Militello, sat down next to Shawcross.

"Hi, Art," Militello said. "You remember we met yesterday when you really helped us out?"

Shawcross nodded.

"Okay, I want you to meet another investigator, William Barnes, who works with us. You want any coffee? Maybe you wanna hit the bathroom before we talk about more things."

"No, I'm okay," Shawcross said.

"Everything is really okay, Art," Militello said. "You did the right thing. I just want you to know that. What you did was okay. Now we need to know about some of the other girls and what went on with them. Maybe you can help us with that and maybe get some of it off your chest."

"I don't know anything about no other girls," Shawcross said.

"Well," Militello began, "you've already admit-

137

ted to us about Gibson, and she was one of the girls we're talking about. Why not get the rest of it off your chest here so you'll feel better by doing that?"

"I still don't know anything about other girls."

Bill Barnes put the picture of Maria Welch in front of Shawcross and said, "Look, why don't you help us find this girl's body? She's got a five-year-old son."

"Don't know her," Shawcross said.

"What about her?" Barnes asked as he put a photo of Darlene Trippi in front of him. "Here we have another girl that's missing. Why don't you help us find both their bodies? Did you know this girl Darlene Trippi?"

"I don't know what you're talking about," Shawcross said to him.

"Look, Art, we believe you're involved with the other girls. How can you explain how we found one earring on June Cicero's body and the other earring from the set in the rented car?" Barnes laid out more photographs in front of Shawcross. "Look at their faces. Were you involved with any of these girls? Do you know anything about what might have happened to them?"

"What are you talking about?" Shawcross asked. "I don't know anything about them. Why do you keep asking me about them?"

"Think about Clara and Rose for a minute here, Art," Charlie Militello said to him. "Just

138

think about them. Why do you want to drag this out? We're going to find out everything eventually anyway. But if you think about them, you can get this over with sooner."

"I still don't know what you're talking about," he said.

They went back and forth for over a half hour until Blythe and Borriello came back into the conference room to spell the team of Militello and Barnes. But Charlie Militello, before he left the room, asked Shawcross if he needed to go to the bathroom. "Maybe you're hungry. Maybe you'd like some coffee. Tell us what you need, Art, and I'll get it for you."

"No, I'm all right and I don't need nothing."

"We're trying to locate Rose for you, Art," Blythe said. "I know you want us to do that."

"Now how can you explain that earring we found in the car, Art?" Len Borriello asked him. "It's identical to the one that we found on the body."

"That earring can come from anywhere. How do I now where it came from?" Art said.

The teams switched again ten minutes later. Militello again asked Shawcross if he needed anything, and again Shawcross told him that he was fine and needed nothing. "But we're still trying to locate Rose, and we have somebody at the nursing home to bring Clara in immediately. You can help us like we're helping you, Art. We're going to find Rose for you. Why don't you tell us what happened?"

"No. I don't know anything about these girls or no earrings," Shawcross said emphatically.

Five minutes later, William Barnes came back into the conference room telling Shawcross that he believed that he was involved with the other girls and laying out the photographs all over again. "Look, look at this picture here. She was the one with the earring? This is the same earring we found in the seat of the car you were driving. Now, look at this picture," he said, pointing to Maria Welch, who was still missing. "What about her?"

But Shawcross said that he didn't recognize the girl with the earring and didn't recognize the girl who they said was still missing.

"Now, look at this photo," Barnes said, pointing to the picture of June Stotts. "Do you recognize her?"

"Yeah," Shawcross said deliberately. "I had lunch with her two or three times at Midtown."

"You know her from the Dunkin' Donuts over on Monroe Avenue?" Barnes asked.

"No," Shawcross said. "Like I told you, I know her from Midtown."

"You ever take her fishing?" Barnes asked.

"No, there was only one girl I took fishing and that was Colleen."

"Colleen?" Barnes began.

140

"Yeah," Shawcross said. "She worked at the Dunkin' Donuts."

"You ever have sex with her?" Militello asked.

"No, we're just friends," Shawcross told them. Then suddenly he looked up and said, "Hey, is Rose coming down?"

"Let me check on that for you, Art," Militello said and left the conference room, leaving Barnes and Shawcross alone for the next ten minutes.

"Look at these four pictures, Art," Barnes began and pointed at Welch, Trippi, Cicero, and Stotts. "Can you explain anything about the earrings so we can understand it?" While Shawcross shook his head and said he didn't know anything, Barnes asked him if he could also help them locate the other two missing women. "If you can find the missing bodies for us, we can get them a proper Christian burial," he said. But Shawcross kept on shaking his head and said that he didn't know anything about the missing women.

For the next half hour, Shawcross and the investigators batted names and photos back and forth across the table. Militello asked him if he remembered Rose having any appointments that day, because they were having trouble finding her at her client's house. Suddenly Shawcross said he remembered that she was taking her patient to the doctor that day. That's where she was. "Okay," Militello said. "We have a guy there at the house. When they get back, he'll bring her here to see

141

you."

But for each exchange of information about Rose or Clara, the detectives held out the possibility that Shawcross could tell them something about one of the women. They were focused and intense, and at one point held up the two earrings in two separate plastic bags, the one found in the car Shawcross was driving, the other found on the body of June Cicero, which was just under the Route 31 bridge where the helicopter had spotted Shawcross sitting outside the passenger side of his car. But Shawcross told them nothing. Then Clara Neal walked in with Dennis Blythe.

Len Borriello turned his attention to Clara. "Look at these earrings, Miss Neal. Do they belong to you?"

"No," Clara said.

"She has nothing to do with this, Art," Borriello said to Shawcross. "Why get her involved? Why don't you tell us the truth?"

"Why are you doing this to me, Artie?" Clara asked him. Then she turned to the police investigators. "You know, maybe these earrings can be anybody's." She left the room and Art said to the three police officers that he'd like to see his wife.

"Let me check on that, Art," Militello said as he left the conference room to see whether Rose had arrived. In the meantime, Barnes and Borriello continued to press Shawcross for an answer

142

about the earrings. "Now we know that they aren't Clara's," they said to him, "we need you to tell us the truth about them."

Twenty minutes later, around 4:30 that afternoon, Militello brought Rose Shawcross into the conference room. She hugged and embraced Art and sat down next to him at the conference table.

"You know I love you, Art," she said. "You know I love you no matter what."

"Listen to Rose, Art," Militello said. "Now, please tell us the truth about all this."

"What really happened, Art?" Rose asked him.

"Well," Art began, "you remember when I came home that time and my eyes were all scratched?"

Rose nodded slowly, but said nothing.

"Well, that time I had to hurt a girl," Shawcross told her.

"Now look what we already have done for you, Art," Militello told him. "We got your wife here to talk to you. We know this is tough, and we got your wife to help you out. Now it's best for everybody here that you tell the truth."

"Artie, no matter what you done," Rose said to her husband, "I'm going to stand behind you the whole time."

The police took her out of the conference room, and when she was gone, Shawcross asked Bill Barnes for the photos of the women again. Barnes handed over the entire stack and asked Shawcross to go through them and pick out the

143

ones that he remembered he was involved with. Art sat down, went through the photos one by one, and carefully placed them in two piles. He arranged the photos of Elizabeth Gibson, Dorothy Blackburn, June Stotts, Patty Ives, June Cicero, Frances Brown, Darlene Trippi, Maria Welch, and Anna Steffen in one pile and the rest of them in another pile. He paused, however, at the photo of Felicia Stephens, as if he didn't know what pile to put it in.

"Why don't we start with the missing girls?" Barnes asked. "Can you tell us where the bodies are that we haven't found?"

"If you can get me a map," Shawcross began, "I can show you."

While Dennis Blythe and Tony Campione left to find maps, Len Borriello put a piece of yellow paper down in front of Shawcross and asked him if he could draw something of a map to help them locate the areas.

A few minutes later, both Blythe and Tony Campione had returned with their map. The police cleared off the large conference table and laid out Campione's large wall map on the surface. Shawcross immediately began to place the murder sites and body dumpsites. "Here's Welch over here," he said, pointing to an area near Island Cottage past the golf course there. "And here's Trippi," he said, running his finger along Redman Road near Clarkson. As he began, Borriello

144

asked Shawcross, "You can take us out and show us where the bodies are, can't you, Art?" He nodded that he would. "And could we bring a stenographer in here to take a full statement from you?" Borriello asked again. "It would be faster than my getting another typewriter in here." Dennis Blythe walked Shawcross to the bathroom before making his statement.

By the time Shawcross had returned, Steven Zinone, the Grand Jury stenographer, had set up his machine in the conference room, and Shawcross slowly and methodically began his confession to the ten prostitute murders in Monroe County and to the murder of Elizabeth Gibson, whose body he'd left in Wayne County. It was a confession he would make over and over again. These were names he would write about a few months later in a diary of his crimes that he put together for his medical investigators and defense team in Wayne County. When the investigators, Barnes, Borriello, Campione, Blythe, and Militello, had finished their formal interrogation of Shawcross for his statement, Zinone packed up his machine and left the conference room. Then the five investigators left the conference room. Everybody needed a break.

It was already after six. Shawcross had been at the police station for almost six and a half hours. Finally, at 6:30, after Shawcross had told police investigator Prescott that he could not identify a photograph of Gail DeRyke and had never been involved with her, Rose Shawcross came back into the conference room.

"You know that VCR we just got from that mail order house?" Arthur asked his wife.

"Yeah?" Rose said.

"Well, I don't think we need it anymore, and I don't want you to have to make the payments," he explained.

"I love you, Art," she said. "I love you and I'm going to stand right by you throughout this entire thing." Shawcross just nodded as Rose continued. "And if you go to prison, I'm going to move to be near you."

"I know," he said.

"I know this is not your fault, Art," Rose said. "It's Vietnam, isn't it?" Shawcross nodded. "It's that Agent Orange, it was those years you spent over there that did this to you. I know you and I know it's not your fault."

"You know the one thing I want you to do for me, Rose?" Art asked.

"What"

"I want you to promise me something."

"What?"

"You can't let my mother find out about this," Shawcross said. "You can't let her find out about this at all."

"All right," Rose said.

"She hasn't said one word to me in seventeen

146

years," Shawcross said to his wife. "Not one word. Ever since I got arrested in Watertown, she hasn't talked to me." He put his head down. Perhaps he was remembering his Christmas present to her and his invitation to visit that was never answered. That was back in January, only weeks before the murder of Dorothy Blackburn. "Not once in seventeen years. And I don't want her to find out about this now."

Chapter 8
"Ask Uncle Sam"

"We're ready to go, Art," Bill Barnes said to Shawcross as the investigators stood outside the door of the conference room. "We're gonna get the elevator."

The five of them stood in front of the elevator and stared at Shawcross, who had just finished confessing to the murders of eleven women. Borriello walked up to him as Shawcross stood there in the hall and, in one swift motion, whipped out a pair of handcuffs from his belt and snapped them on Art's wrists in front. Shawcross was now in custody. It was the law. There were no words. There didn't have to be. Shawcross simply assumed the position he had assumed throughout most of his life and allowed himself to be handcuffed by the police. At least they were humane about it; they cuffed him in front.

Now, instead of asking him to accompany them to the car, they were escorting him to the elevator and into the garage, a police officer on either side of him, guiding him wherever they wanted him to go. That morning, when Shawcross had unlocked his bike from the rack, he was ostensibly a free man: "Will you talk to us, Art?" "Will you ride with us down to the station?" "You don't have to do anything you don't want to do, Art." "Won't you cooperate with us? It's been great because you've been so helpful." And now, by seven in the evening, the thank-you's had stopped. He was a prisoner again, just as he'd been for almost all his life, especially since he'd got off the plane from Vietnam. But for Shawcross, the cuffs on his hands and the police holding onto him from either side were only the physical evidence of his having been a psychological prisoner his entire life, even years before he'd gone to Vietnam. I would soon meet Arthur Shawcross myself and get to know exactly what kind of prisoner he had been.

Dennis Blythe led Shawcross to the left side of Deputy Chief Terrance Rickard's car. Rickard had been one of the officers in charge of the serial killer task force. Then Blythe climbed in the right rear seat, next to his prisoner. Bill Barnes got into the front seat, while Len Borriello slid himself behind the wheel and started the car.

"We'd like you to direct us to where you picked up Welch," Blythe said to Shawcross. "And where you did her and dumped her body. Just take us the way you went."

"Okay," Shawcross said to Borriello. "Get on

Lake Avenue and start driving in the direction of Charlotte."

They passed the Maplewood YMCA on Lake Avenue and Borriello tried to turn his head around to see Shawcross. "This where you took Patricia Ives?" he asked over his shoulder.

"Yeah," Shawcross said. Might as well fill in the details and give them the guided tour. He might not be seeing the outside of prison for the rest of his life.

They drove by Turning Point Park and Bill Barnes swung around in the front seat and said, "And this is where Stotts was."

"This is the turn right here," Borriello chimed in.

"Oh, no," Shawcross volunteered. "Not this turn, the next one."

And they drove along Lake Avenue to the intersection of Beach, where Shawcross suddenly said, "Turn left right here," and Borriello swung the car onto Beach Avenue.

"You ever go smelting here, Art?" Barnes asked him, more in the way of conversation than for any other reason.

"Nah," Shawcross said, trying to lapse back into the easy conversation he'd had with the cops before they'd slapped the cuffs on him. "Don't do smelts." The car cruised slowly along Beach until Shawcross said, "When you get to the restaurant up here, you got to bear left."

"Okay, I know where to go from there," Borriello

said as they passed Schaeller's Restaurant.

"Now slow down," Art said, "and go to the second set of arrow signs and stop." The car rolled to a slow stop. "Right here. I dumped her body here. See? Over by those two trees back there." He tried to point out the window into the darkness of the surrounding woods with his cuffed hands. The windows were already steaming up inside the car. The temperature outside was dropping fast.

"Let's get out," Blythe said. "Art, can you get out and show us to the spot?" All the cops got out and Blythe opened Shawcross's door and helped him out of the car. He handed him a flashlight and indicated that he could start walking. "You lead, we'll follow," he said. Shawcross began walking through the heavy brush, which was cold and damp even against their coats. The police followed him for about four minutes as the foliage around him grew denser and denser. Finally he pushed aside a clump of bushes between two tall trees and pointed to a light spot on the ground with the flashlight.

"There she is," he said as the other officers came up behind him.

About five minutes later more police officers arrived and the four investigators and their prisoner took off for Redman Road in the deputy chief's car.

"Now, how can I get to Redman Road from here, Art?" Borriello asked him, turning around so

151

he could see Shawcross over his shoulder.

"Don't know," Shawcross answered. "I can't give no directions, really."

"Well how'd you get there that night?" Borriello asked again. Sometimes he really didn't believe how this guy got around at all. Imagine eluding the police for two years—and he was just riding around on a bicycle most of the time.

"Took 104," Shawcross said as Borriello drove along Island Cottage Road to Latta to Manitou and from there to Ridge Road, which was County 104. "Then you got to go to the next set of lights after the one ahead. That's Redman."

"When did you think about killing each of these girls, Art?" Investigator Barnes asked him. "I mean, did you decide to kill them right away when you got ahold of them? Did you go right after them? Did you immediately get a strong hold on them?"

"Yeah, that's what I done," Shawcross said. "I went right to kill them when I got 'em around the neck."

"Now, after you killed them, Art," Barnes continued, "did you ever talk to 'em?"

"How do you talk to a dead person?" Shawcross asked him with a completely straight face, as if he were the cop and Barnes were the killer.

Barnes kept right after him. Their conversation was almost surrealistic in the winter darkness. "Where did you keep them after you killed them,

Art?"

"Right in the front seat," he answered.

"And how did you pick your dumpsites?" Barnes continued.

"I just drove around," he said. "Where there weren't no people around."

"Now what about the river gorge?" Barnes asked.

"That's right where it happened," Shawcross said. "Where I did it."

"And you weren't ever afraid of being stopped by the police?" Barnes asked almost incredulously, but without betraying any emotion.

Many police officers at the mop-up stage of a serial murder investigation are amazed at how easily the killer seems to slip in and out of the shadows. In Shawcross's case, he was able to cruise through the Lake Avenue district in two different cars for two years before the police managed to find a witness who put him in the district among the prostitutes. The same witness enabled the police to put one of the victims right in his car on the day before she was discovered. When they confronted him with that clue, his admission to the crime followed almost immediately. When they searched the car they found the clue that led to the next admission and from there to the rest of the murders. But during the entire two-year period, Borriello realized, Shawcross was going back and forth on a bike at times when most people were at home in bed and no one even seemed to notice him.

When the magnitude of his crimes became clear—and it had yet to become clear to Borriello as he drove his suspect through the darkness along the banks of the Genesee River—it was the ease of it all that seemed to make the strongest impression. How did Shawcross manage to get away with it? How did he manage to drive around with all these dead bodies in his car? Why was it that while he was driving Maria Welch from Lake Avenue to her final grave in that clump of bushes alongside Beach Avenue not one person saw them? And he had done it eleven times. At least, it was eleven times that the police knew about.

"That's it, right here," Shawcross called out from the blackness of the rear seat. "No, it's up ahead, by those houses. Slow down up here by the bridge." Borriello allowed the car to coast and slowly rolled up to the bridge. "Now stop right here."

"So where's the body?" they asked him.

Shawcross pointed with both hands at a spot between two yellow reflective markers alongside the bridge. "It's right there," he said.

The three investigators piled out of the car with their flashlights but couldn't find a thing. "You got to get out and help us, Art," Blythe said as he opened Shawcross's door and helped him out. Shawcross walked over to the side of the culvert,

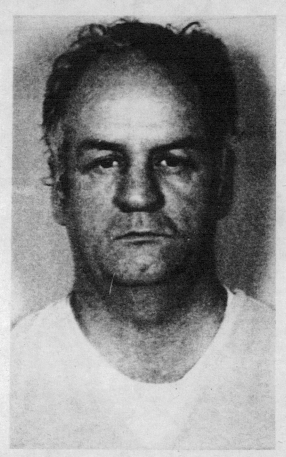

Arthur Shawcross was arraigned on January 5, 1990 on eight separate counts of second-degree murder. He would finally be convicted of eleven murders. (*Courtesy of AP/Wide World Photos*)

The seventh grade class photo of Arthur Shawcross. He is fourth from the left in the top row. *(Courtesy of the Gannett Rochester Newspapers)*

Sheriff's deputies in Watertown, New York escort convicted murderer Arthur Shawcross to prison for the deaths of Karen Ann Hill and Jack Blake in 1972. *(Courtesy of AP/Wide World Photos)*

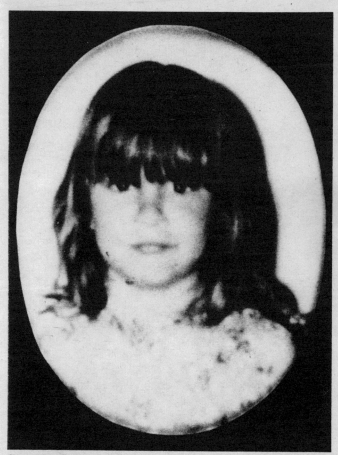

Karen Ann Hill was eight years old when Shawcross brutally raped her, then suffocated her to death. (*Courtesy of the Gannett Rochester Newspapers*)

Jack O. Blake was the first child victim of Arthur Shawcross. He was eleven years old when he died. (*Courtesy of the Gannett Rochester Newspapers*)

The building on Alexander Street where Shawcross shared an apartment with his fourth wife, Rose Walley Shawcross, during his two-year killing spree. (*Courtesy of the Gannett Rochester Newspapers*)

Prior to his arrest, Arthur Shawcross appeared to be a quiet, solitary man who worked hard and liked to fish and hunt. (*Courtesy of the Gannett Rochester Newspapers*)

Linda Neary was Shawcross's second wife.
(Courtesy of the Gannett Rochester Newspapers)

THE VICTIMS*

Patricia Ives, 25, found adjacent to the river gorge behind the Maplewood YMCA.

Frances Brown, 22, found on the river's east bank near Seth Green Drive.

June Cicero, 34, found in a culvert under Route 31 near Northampton.

Darlene Trippi, 32, found after Shawcross lead police to her body in a remote area off Redman Road in the town of Clarkson.

Anna Marie Steffen, 28, found in the Genesee River gorge area near 740 Lake Ave.

*(Courtesy of the Gannett Rochester Newspapers)

Dorothy Blackburn, 27, found in
Salmon Creek in Northampton Park.

June Stotts, 30, found in
Turning Point Park near the river gorge.

Maria Welch, 22, found after Shawcross
led police to her body in a remote area off
Edgemere Drive near Lake Ontario.

Elizabeth Gibson, found by a
hunter in a remote area of Wayne County.

Dorothy Keller, 59, found on
Seth Green Island in the river gorge.

Police remove the frozen body of Darlene Trippi from a small creek along Redman Road in the town of Clarkson. (*Courtesy of the Gannett Rochester Newspapers*)

Police photographer takes a picture, at the scene, of the body of Frances Brown. *(Courtesy of the Gannett Rochester Newspapers)*

Charles Siragusa was the district attorney who prosecuted Arthur Shawcross. (*Courtesy of the Gannett Rochester Newspapers*)

The investigation and trial of Arthur Shawcross was probably one of the best documented cases in recent criminal history. Here Shawcross and his attorney view one of his many taped confessions. (*Courtesy of the Gannett Rochester Newspapers*)

under the bridge, and between the markers, and pointed them right to the body of Darlene Trippi. It was just a little after eight in the evening. Then Shawcross and Borriello returned to the police car while they waited for Blythe and Barnes to join them by the rear fender.

"You know, Art," Len Borriello said, "you went to great lengths to hide the bodies." Shawcross nodded. "Isn't it true," he continued, "that you did this so that if they weren't found for a period of time, it would be difficult to place you with the victims?"

"Yeah," Shawcross said almost nonchalantly.

"Well, you killed a lot of people," the detective said. "Weren't you afraid of ever getting caught by the police?"

"I guess that I really didn't think about it," Shawcross told him, and left the investigator to think about the magnitude of the crimes and the circumstances that had led the police to Shawcross in the first place just the day before. As it was with most serial killers, the evidence that connects the killer to the crimes usually doesn't fall into place until after the killer is identified.

"Well," Borriello continued as if he were trying to put together pieces for a research project, "did you ever tell anyone else about anything you've done?"

"Nope," Shawcross said, just as laconic and closed up as he'd been even while confessing to all the homicides he said he'd committed.

Having been shown the dumpsites of the missing women's bodies, the investigators put Shawcross back in the car and drove back toward the Public Safety Building in Rochester. It was almost 8:30, and Shawcross would not be going home again. On the way back into town, Borriello drove down Colby Street, past the location where Felicia Stephens' body had been found earlier that day. As they neared the spot, Dennis Blythe turned to Shawcross, who was sitting next to him, and asked, "Know why we're driving along this street, Art?"

"Nope," Shawcross answered almost abstractedly. But then, as the car passed the exact spot where they had discovered her body, Blythe noticed that Shawcross did a double-take, as if he recognized the area and it surprised him. Dennis Blythe didn't say anything about it for the rest of the trip. It would wait, he told himself; it would all come out later.

The three detectives who rode with Shawcross were joined back in the fourth floor conference room of the Public Safety Building by Investigators Militello and Campione, who had been following them all along in Militello's unit. They put Shawcross back in the room and took off the cuffs, then Campione asked him if he wanted something to eat or a cup of coffee.

"You wanna use the bathroom, Art?" Tony asked him.

156

While Shawcross shook his head no, Charlie Militello asked him again if there was anything he wanted and assured him that they wanted to help him. "You know you did the right thing, Art, by showing us what you did and confessing. It was the absolute right thing."

"I want to ask you about the Felicia Stephens girl, Art," Tony Campione began. "You know we found her right near where we discovered June Cicero and Dorothy Blackburn over in the creek and that in all likelihood the cause of Stephens' death will be the same as Cicero's and Blackburn's."

"Yeah, and besides," Charlie Militello chimed in, "her clothing. It was tossed along the roadside near where the body was found, just like the other two girls'. And she was killed in the exact same way, I bet."

"I told you guys before," Shawcross said emphatically. "She was black. You asked me that already. I don't do black women. I didn't go with any black girls."

"You know we treated you good, Art," Militello said. "We got Clara for you. We got you Rose when you asked us, and we been honest with you. My bosses asked me why you didn't tell us the truth about Felicia Stephens. They asked me that and I couldn't answer."

"But I told you that I don't do black girls," Shawcross repeated.

157

"That won't wash, Art," Militello continued. "The circumstances were just too similar. I know you killed her, and I'm going to have to explain to my bosses why you aren't telling the truth about Stephens." He paused and looked at his watch. "Well, it's already after nine and you're tired, I know, and I'm tired. But it doesn't matter. I'm just going to try to explain to my bosses that you done real good and that I'm not mad at you." He left the conference room before Shawcross could answer.

"Art," Tony Campione said as he walked in almost immediately after Militello had left, "I can't understand it at all. We had all been good to you. This Stephens girl was almost exactly like all the rest we covered today, and her body was in the same park where the two other bodies were discovered. Now, you have to put yourself into my shoes for a minute here. Make believe that you're Investigator Campione and I'm Arthur Shawcross. Would you believe it if I said to you that I wouldn't do it? Would you believe it especially after you saw two others that I did in the same place that were exactly like the one I said I wouldn't do?"

Shawcross didn't answer.

"Now, you know what's happening right now, probably." Campione continued. "Investigator Militello's probably getting chewed out because you haven't been truthful."

Five minutes later Len Borriello walked into the

conference room and went straight over to Shawcross as if they were all members of the same club. "Art," he said in an astonished voice, as if he couldn't believe what was happening. "What happened with Investigator Militello? Why didn't you tell him the truth? I just heard him getting chewed out by the bosses. Jeez, it's awful."

"She didn't even get in the car," Shawcross said.

"Then how can you explain what happened to her?" Borriello asked as Dennis Blythe walked back into the conference room, stood there, and listened as Shawcross completed his explanation of the Felicia Stephens homicide.

"See, I was driving down Plymouth Avenue to Main Street," Shawcross continued. "It was about 2 A.M. on the Wednesday, or maybe it was the Thursday, after Christmas. I was stopped in the gray Chevrolet at that red light at the intersection of Main and Plymouth with my right front window about halfway down when this black girl stuck her head right into the car. I put up the automatic window on her side and I caught her throat in the window. I reached over with both hands and choked her while she was screaming rape. Then I lowered the window, grabbed her by her hair, and dragged her into the car. I pulled her in right through the window, finished choking her, and drove up to the expressway. I drove all the way to Northampton Park, where I just dumped her body. I remember that she was wearing gray boots, three

159

pairs of pants, and a rust-colored long corduroy coat. I stripped her down."

"Why did you take off her clothes?" Campione asked him.

"I just wanted to take a look at her," Shawcross answered.

"Where did you put Stephens' body?" Blythe asked.

"Into a small hole," Shawcross said. "Like a foundation on Colby Street. I threw her coat on top of her and took the first left to get back to the city. While I was driving away and nobody could see me, I threw her pants out the driver's side window onto the side of the road. Then I grabbed her boots and did the same thing. As I got back into the city, off the expressway, I saw that there was more of her clothing inside the car. I drove over behind the War Memorial on Court Street and tossed them over the north side of the bridge."

With the Felicia Stephens case now closed, the investigators first assumed that the deaths of some of the other black prostitutes in the area might be cleared up by Arthur Shawcross confessions. This was a completely reasonable assumption in light of what Shawcross had told them about Stephens, even though the Stephens case, if taken only on the basis of Shawcross's statements, was more a matter of chance than the other killings.

Shawcross told the police that not only did he *not* seek out Stephens, but because she did not fit the profile of the women he had killed, he had sought to avoid her rather than kill her. The homicide itself was different because Shawcross didn't have sex with her and didn't kill her because of his inability to have sex. He killed her, he said, precisely because he didn't want to have an encounter with her. When she screamed, she became like the other victims who had threatened to expose him. His dumping her body in Northampton Park was a matter of his familiarity with the area.

However, having confessed to the Felicia Stephens murder, Shawcross opened the door to the possibility that he had killed other black prostitutes as well, and police investigators sought his confession in the Kim Logan and Rosalie Oppel slayings for the next few hours. Shawcross reiterated that not only was he not responsible for the murders of the black prostitutes in the area, he had committed the Stephens murder only because she'd stuck her head in his car and he'd tried to get away. Shawcross stuck to his story and finally said that if necessary, he would take a polygraph test to determine whether his refusals to confess to the Logan and Oppel murders were truthful. The police finally dropped their attempts to get his confessions and turned to learning about how Shawcross gained control of the crime scene and was able to lure his victims into danger.

Shawcross kept telling the police that the women who he killed were victims of opportunity. They either appeared at his car, got into his car while it was open, went swimming with him in the creek, or knew him from previous encounters. He said that the women were more in shock over what he did to them than fearful, and that by the time they realized he was killing them, they were too weak to resist. Most of the women, Shawcross said, had made fun of his inability to get an erection or to maintain an erection, and some had threatened to tell the police that he'd raped them when he'd tried to get his money back.

Toward the end of the evening, just before midnight, when he was led up to Booking, Investigator Coleman asked Shawcross if he thought that what he had done to the girls was terrible.

"Yes, it was," Shawcross said. "These were terrible things I did. I simply can't control my urge to kill."

"What should we do with you, Art?" Coleman asked. "What should the police do?"

"You have to put me in jail for the rest of my life," Shawcross said. "You put me away, because if I'm ever released, just as sure as you're sitting here I'm going to kill again."

"Art, I want you to meet police Lieutenant Edward Grant," Investigator Terry Coleman said to Shawcross after another visit from Rose had ended. "Eat your dinner, Art," she had told him as she

162

was leaving. "And don't worry, I'll stand beside you no matter where they send you." But Shawcross was not of a mind to eat. He stared at the chicken wings and salad on the conference table in front of him after Rose left and didn't touch them. It was only a few minutes before eleven and Shawcross had been in custody and under interrogation for almost twelve hours. Now there was a new guy who wanted to stick his gloved finger deep into Shawcross's brain to see what made it tick and what made him kill. Shawcross was beginning to feel like a caged animal in a zoo.

"I would like to talk to you about some of the crime scenes," Grant said. "I want to know if that's okay with you." Shawcross nodded. He really didn't know what he was supposed to say. Even when he said he was telling the truth, they didn't believe him. He might just as well open up and let them in. They'd be in for the rest of his life and he knew it. Maybe there'd be something in it for him if he cooperated. He didn't know.

"It would help me," Grant continued, "to better understand the crime scenes if you talked to me about them. Answered some of my questions."

"How's that going to help me?" Shawcross asked.

"Well," and Grant paused, "it's not really going to help you. But it will help other police officers in their interpretations of other crime scenes. Now you know you're under absolutely no obligation to talk to me about this at all. You have an absolute right to remain silent and the right to an attorney and a right to have that attorney right here while you're being questioned if you want. Now, do you understand these rights that I've just explained?" Shawcross nodded. "And do you consent to talk to me about this even after I've explained these rights?"

"Yeah," Shawcross said while he nodded. He'd answer whatever they wanted as long as it was true. But he was still feeling embarrassed, not only about his crimes but about the levels of violence associated with them. Shawcross had already told Terry Coleman how he'd had thirty-nine unconfirmed kills in Vietnam with his M-16. He described them. He'd said that he was alone in the bush for long periods and made most of the kills when he was moving ammo from firebase to firebase.

"You ever kill any women?" Coleman had asked him.

"Yeah, two," Shawcross said. "One was a young girl, the other was a teenager. They were both VC. I mutilated them."

Maybe it was those visions of what he had said he'd done in Vietnam that had been playing in his mind during the murders. That's what Rose Shawcross had attributed it to. He had learned how to elude the VC patrols, he said, while he was killing in Vietnam, and he had certainly learned how to elude the police patrols while he was killing

164

in Rochester. He didn't brag about it; he stated it as a matter of fact. All his killings were a matter of fact. They were clean and they were silent. One could almost say that if Shawcross had the history in Vietnam he claimed to have, then his killings in Rochester could be replays of what was going on in his mind. Or maybe not. That's what Ed Grant had to try to find out in the hours immediately after Shawcross's arrest and before his booking. These interviews would be the first steps in trying to determine exactly what made Shawcross kill and keep on killing even when the police were sitting just two seats away from him at the Dunkin' Donuts, describing the case.

"You knew Dorothy Blackburn?" Grant asked. "She was victim number one."

"I knew her," Shawcross.

"Why'd you kill her?" he asked.

"She bit me!" Shawcross said with a hostility that one might almost believe justified the killing in his mind as an act of self-defense. "I choked her."

"You bit her also?" Grant asked. The police knew there were severe bite marks on Blackburn's body and that part of her vagina had been torn out.

"No," Shawcross said. "She bit me."

And that's how it went — with Anna Steffen: "I got into an argument about her being pregnant and swimming in the river and I strangled her and dumped her down a bank"; Dorothy Keller: "She was a friend of mine who came to the apartment. I got into an argument with her because she used to steal food from me and I asked her, 'Why did you steal food from me when I give you money?' and she said she would tell the police I raped her, so I beat her on the back of her head with a stick, moved her twenty feet off the path, and left her there. Then I came back and flipped her skull away with a stick"; Patty Ives: "I used to see her a lot of times. We was having sex behind the YMCA and she wouldn't stop screaming and there were kids right there who would hear us, so I strangled her right there, sat her up, and left her there"; Frances Brown: "She broke the gearshift in the Dodge Omni, and I got mad and she said she would tell the police that she knew who I was, so I strangled her and dumped over the riverbank where fishermen set up their tables"; June Stotts: "I known her for a long time from eating together with her, and she knew Rose. She was slow, a retarded girl. She told me she was a virgin, but when we had sex she didn't bleed or nothing, and we had a fight and then she said that she was going to tell Rose and tell the police I raped her when I didn't rape her. I strangled her, dumped her clothes in the barge canal, put her on the riverbank between some pieces of rug, then came back and cut her open right down the front so she'd decompose faster"; June Cicero: "She wised off to me and said 'I know who

166

you are,' and that I was the killer, so I had to kill her. I dumped her in a snowbank on the creek under the bridge, and when I went back a few weeks later to see if she'd been found yet, the helicopter spotted me."

Now Grant was truly fascinated. "So you spent time with these girls before you killed them?" he asked.

"I knew 'em all and they knew me," Shawcross said.

"Would you say you were a familiar face on the street, to these girls, and to the whole community that they frequented?"

"That's right. That's what you could say," Shawcross answered. "Some of the girls even gave me my money back when I couldn't come when we were having sex."

"You knew how to move around the neighborhoods," Ed Grant suggested. "But how were you able to kill these girls so easily?"

"Because they knew me and they never expected it. I struck quickly, and they were always in shock at first. They didn't know what I was doing," Shawcross said.

"Where did you learn to do that?" Grant asked him.

"Ask Uncle Sam!" Shawcross said.

"Does that mean you learned this in the military?" Grant followed up.

"Ask Uncle Sam!"

After asking Shawcross about his sexual problems and learning that he couldn't have orgasms because of pain in his left testicle as well as psychological problems, Grant asked him whether he had any fascination with the cases of the murdered prostitutes after he had heard about them on the news or read about them in the papers.

"No," Shawcross said. "I didn't follow 'em in the news. I didn't think about 'em."

"Did you talk about them with the police at all?" Grant asked. "Did you see yourself as playing a game with the police as they pursued the killer?"

"No," Shawcross said. "I'd sit in the Dunkin' Donuts all the time while the police were there—they go there a lot—and I'd listen to 'em talk. Sometimes I'd even ask them about the cases and they'd tell me what they knew and where they thought the case was goin'. That's how I knew the girl they'd found."

"So was this like a game for you?" Grant asked.

"No," he said. "It was just like business as usual."

"Tell me about where you learned to cut up bodies so they'd decompose faster," Grant asked.

"Ask Uncle Sam," Shawcross replied.

Chapter 9
Pathologica Fantastica

What is the real truth about Arthur Shawcross? Not even Shawcross himself understood it, or, if he thought he did, was willing to admit it. No one, not the Army psychiatrist who spoke to him after his return from Vietnam, not the prison psychologists at Green Haven, not the therapists in Broome County after he was paroled, probably understood what Shawcross was. And yet this was the man I had to build a medical defense for in Wayne County.

As he was shuffled back and forth from his cell at the Monroe County lockup in those hot days of July, months before his first trial, I began my research into Shawcross's background, his obvious symptoms of a variety of medical, psychological, biosocial, and other disorders, I began to feel that there was also something else at work in this man's background, something so big and so severe it might easily be either missed or called something else.

Here was a person who had been through years

of therapy both in and out of prison and who had been evaluated medically by institution after institution, including the United States Army. Yet here was a man who in specific emotional states was a virtual killing machine, who could go from committing a murder with his own bare hands and dumping his victim on a cold, desolate spot on the Genesee River gorge to his psychotherapist's couch the next day without displaying a trace of remorse or conflict. In fact, he began his killing spree while he was under the active supervision of the New York State Parole Board and a bevy of psychological counselors and social workers. How could this have happened? Part of my assignment was to find the answer and to document my findings.

It would not be until I'd finished most of my research, interviewed Arthur Shawcross about his feelings, memories, thoughts, and impressions, read the reports and viewed actual interviews of other medical and psychological professionals, and spoken with members of his family and people who knew him that a composite picture finally began to form. The more I thought about it, the more I couldn't shake my belief that Shawcross, among all the other things that had affected him, was also suffering from one of the most severe cases of cumulative post-traumatic stress that I had ever seen or heard about. His post-traumatic stress, I believe, was related to a series of events which, according to his own account—which has not been independently confirmed — began when he was a small child and continued right through to the very day he committed his final murder. It will no doubt continue right through the rest of his life, which he will, if his sentence is fully carried out, spend behind bars.

His post-traumatic stress was so pervasive that it left him in a state of "emotional anesthesia," psychologically numb, unable to relate to anyone within a normal, functional framework. By the time I began my interviews, he was an individual with only two basic states of existence: homicidal and nonhomicidal. In the former state he was a terrifying, almost inhuman monster. In his nonhomicidal state he was an emotionally diminished, almost passive creature. It was as if he were drugged. I believed Shawcross may have been predisposed to the development of this severe post-traumatic stress disorder by a preexisting psychopathological, biochemical, neurological, and possibly genetic condition. The medical research that I coordinated and reviewed told me I was probably correct. It allowed me to get inside the mind of Arthur Shawcross, one of the worst serial killers ever to afflict the people of New York State.

But why should we penetrate this man's mind, now that he is behind bars again? Other crimes capture the headlines and become features on the tabloid news shows. Since the Shawcross case was tried in early 1991 and he was sent to prison, we

171

have news stories about the alleged torture/mutilation/murders of Jeffrey Dahmer in Wisconsin, Ohio, and possibly other jurisdictions; the confessions in Mississippi of Donald Evans, whom the press is calling the "worst" serial killer in history, and the return of accused serial killer Charles Ng to face the death penalty in California.

Society at large can easily dismiss Arthur Shawcross because he should no longer be a threat to anyone on the outside. However, neither the medical profession nor the legal profession can dismiss him. His case red-flags too many of our own mistakes and signals issues in dealing with people like Shawcross *before* and not *after* they kill. The issue now is prevention, and that's why we need to find out as much as we can about Arthur Shawcross. That's why Lieutenant Edward Grant interviewed Shawcross about crime scenes and body disposition as extensively as he did *after* the latter confessed to the eleven murders in Monroe and Wayne Counties. He wasn't simply trying to get more information in order to hang the guy; the police officer needed to know how and why Shawcross did what he did so that the police would be in a better position to recognize the indicators of other serial killers in future crime scene investigations. Unless the police fully understand the magnitude of what they're dealing with, they won't be able to protect us from the devastation of serial and spree killers.

172

But the police are not alone in their need for information. Parole and probation officers also need all the help the medical profession can give them because they are, in reality, our first line of defense against serial killers. They deal with serial killers before they become serial killers. Most of these murderers are repeat offenders. Most have been through the system so many times they know the rules better than the people in corrections and law enforcement. Their probation officers have handled them in the past and are charged with their management and supervision when they return to the outside world. Most repeat violent offenders do, in fact, return to the outside world before they commit the ultimate crimes that will either send them to the executioner's block or put them in prison for life. Therefore probation officers should know what goes on in the minds of serial killers and spree murderers before they begin their final phase so that they can at least get them into some kind of treatment to defuse the time bombs before they go off.

The Arthur Shawcross case was supervised for almost twenty years by the New York State Division of Parole. In fact, he was one of the more supervised parolees over the course of his travels to and from prison, yet he still became one of the worst killers in the state's history. Why? The parole and probation system should have protected us against Shawcross, but it did not. In fact, the local

Rochester newspapers reported that the probation division actually "hid" Arthur Shawcross in the city of Rochester after officials in communities of Binghamton, Vestal, Delhi, and Fleishmanns learned of his identity and his past and pursued him. In Rochester, parole officials assumed, he could achieve the anonymity necessary to reestablish himself and rejoin society. Instead, with his old triggers still in place, he simply resumed his interrupted career as a serial killer. Was his release and management a case of negligence of the highest order, or was it tragically a matter of 'professionals' not recognizing or comprehending what they were looking at? I fully believe it was the latter, because most people don't understand why serial and spree murderers kill.

The real story of Arthur Shawcross challenges our belief systems because the deeper we go, the more we find ourselves wrapped up in Shawcross's own violent fantasies. His visions of terror and brutality become the reality and, if we let ourselves, we actually can see each of the homicides from his point of view. We have to be careful, lest they, however terrible and unjustified by any moral standard, begin to make rational sense.

Prostitutes like Dorothy Blackburn who bit him or scratched him were strangled to death in an act of "self-defense," he told investigators. Prostitutes like Liz Gibson who tried to steal his money were killed. Prostitutes like Darlene Trippi who made

174

fun of him were killed. Women who deceived him and threatened him with exposure, like June Stotts and Maria Welch, were not only killed, they were mutilated. And he killed a black woman named Felicia Stephens simply because he was afraid of sexual relations with blacks. Black inmates at Attica, he said, had raped him. Felicia Stephens stuck her head through Shawcross's car window and was asphyxiated when he closed it across her throat. To listen to his explanation, it was almost an instinctive act of self-preservation. His actions and the actions of most serial killers and spree murderers are too instinctive and too primitive to be dismissed as mere crimes. They are something else.

When we spoke to Arthur Shawcross and read his written journal of his experiences, the tales he told us were unbelievable in their violence and human degradation. No human being, we assumed, could have endured what Shawcross had endured at the hands of others. By the time he amalgamated his stories of his own abuse with the recountings of his homicides, a composite picture emerged of a person who either believed he had a right to commit these crimes or a person who was so locked up within his own fantasy that he was only dimly aware of reality. Shawcross, we found, had spent much of his adult life in a dream state, only vaguely responding to the stimuli of the outside world. That's what had made him seem so passive to psychologists at Green Haven. They knew something was troubling him, but because he seemed to be recovering from his violent rages, they assumed that he was adjusting to prison life and becoming rehabilitated. On the surface it might have been a plausible assumption. However, throughout the entire period, we came to discover after he committed his crimes, he was reliving either the "truth" or his fantasies of his experiences in Vietnam which, if taken at face value, are more violent and gory than any low-budget horror movie.

When an individual lives with his fantasies to the extent that they *become* a reality that is built into the fabric of his personal history, that individual could be diagnosed as suffering from a variety of disorders including disassociative disorder, paranoia and the like. People who suffer from these conditions usually cannot distinguish their fantasies from reality because the two have become one. They are not having delusions or hallucinations, they are simply living out the fantasies that their minds have created for them, a kind of denial of reality in the most severe extreme. Most serial killers experience this phenomenon from time to time in their lives.

I now believe that Shawcross suffered from a condition that I term pathologica fantastica. That is, experiences, real or imagined, of so wide-ranging a nature and intensity as to prevent any conventional psychological professional from creating a consistent profile of subject's disorder.

176

Combined with such medical conditions krypto-pyroluria or medical cannibalism and poisoning and severe brain damage from his head injuries, Shawcross's mental state made him more than unfit to live on his own recognizance on the outside of an institution. It made him into a ticking time bomb on a very short fuse. It took only his perception of rejection by his family and his perception of being attacked by the prostitutes along Lake Avenue to set him off. And when he went off, he didn't stop until the police picked him up for loitering around the corpse of one of his most recent victims.

This was the same way he had been identified seventeen years earlier, after he had just started a skein of serial killings in Watertown in which cannibalism and necrophilia, he told psychiatrists, were also factors. Was Shawcross deliberately trying to get caught? Had he deliberately tried to get caught seventeen years before, when he'd returned to the burial site? These were just some of the issues we also had to face as we assembled the material for our medical investigation into the causes of Shawcross's crimes.

Arthur Shawcross, who is only 44 years old, presented us with one of the most completely documented histories of an individual who has spent most of his adult life in penal institutions. He also presented us with vivid descriptions of child abuse, wartime experiences, and prison experiences which, even if he only *believes* them to be true, amount to nothing less than a lifelong nightmare of blood and absolute terror.

In order to deal with the feelings that his possible "fantasies" arouse, I must usually deal with them as realities. That is, what they seem like to the killers who suffer from them, and is what they must be to anyone who attempts to talk to the killers they are interviewing. Therefore, we will many times refer to the most fantastic and improbable stories as realities—not because we believe them to be one hundred percent true, but because the killer believes them to be true and we can reach him only through the levels of his fantasy. Of course, my experience has also shown me that sometimes the most unlikely fantasies turn out to be true after all.

In Shawcross's case, his fantasies do not seem to vary widely in the major details from interview to interview. He will lie consistently to protect himself from having to reveal shameful facts about what he did to some of the corpses. Sometimes he seems to invent more horrific acts to make his crimes seem worse than they are, but sometimes he will not mention key facts about the crimes when they truly are horrific. At first, for example, Shawcross routinely denied performing any cannibalistic acts on his victims to the police. Investigators knew that the bodies had been mutilated and that, given the state of decomposition of the corpses, it could only have been the killer or someone who visited the corpse afterward who mutilated them. Yet Shawcross denied it. Later, however, in a journal written for his medical investigators, he revealed some of the cannibalistic acts that he performed. Similarly, in letters written about his first set of killings, he revealed acts of cannibalism that he performed on them as well. These may indeed have been fantasies that we need to take at face value, as if they are real.

If they are real to the killer, they must have some reality for his interviewers, because the killer is often acting on his fantasies *as if* they are real.

Chapter 10
Shawcross Corners

"After I was first introduced to sex by my Aunt Tina, my mother's sister, I became obsessed with sex. I was very upset when my aunt went back home. I was about nine then."

That's how Shawcross began the journal he wrote for the psychologists and medical investigators researching his background prior to his trial in Wayne County, New York, for the murder of his eleventh victim. It was his first experience with sex, he said, and it came when he was most vulnerable, just after a time when Shawcross experienced a dramatic change within his family. When he was about eight or nine, the innocence of a secure household was ripped out from under him when his father was accused of having fathered a child in Australia during World War Two. His mother turned on both his father and him, and Shawcross was from that moment on shut out of his parents' lives.

"Things were fine up until I was eight, nine years old," Shawcross told Dr. Park Deitz, the psychiatrist for the prosecution. "Then my father's mother, as far as I can recall, got a letter from some woman in Australia stating that she was married to my father and had a boy child, you know. And then my grandmother, my father's mother, I don't know why, but she gave this letter to my mother and from that moment, Dad couldn't watch TV, you know. He wouldn't go nowhere, didn't go nowhere. If he was caught looking at another woman, Mom would throw something at him or threaten him or whatever. Cursed him out in two or three different languages. And I looked up to my father up until that moment, I'd see my father walk around with his head down all of the time and sometimes it would get so bad that Dad would walk out of the house or go down the cellar or go out in the garage. It bugged me. I couldn't understand it growing up. I think it just stuck with me. I just couldn't handle it."

Shawcross said that not only did he lose all respect for his father as a man at that time, but that the entire family suffered. Their lives simply shut down and they went into free-fall.

"My father wasn't . . . my father. Usually a kid growing up goes to talk to his father. I think I was more ashamed of my father from then on. . . . He just quit being the father figure in the house. My mother, she bossed everybody. . . . He could have had a good job where he was working. He could have went up in grade and made more money. He

181

could have had an office job, but my mother hounded him over the years and he just stuck away in the gravel pit somewhere. I imagine she had people checking on him to see if he was still in the gravel pit. I know sometimes when in the wintertime he had to go plow snow, they told Dad, 'You have to plow snow,' he couldn't tell them no. And every time he would come home, she accused him of this or that and just fighting. Argument all night long, cursing, and it's hard to grow up like that. . . . She told him 'If I ever caught you with another woman, I will kill you.' I remember that. She would be standing there in the house with a knife in her hands or something, saying 'If I catch you with another woman or looking at another woman, I will kill you.' "

Nothing his father could do earned him any respect in Shawcross's eyes. Arthur told his doctors over and over again that his father gave up on his own manhood and Arthur was shamed and humiliated by it. Even to this very day, he reveals, a man who can't perform as a man is a shameful thing. "I am very ashamed of my father for carrying on his life the way he did. I regret that we didn't have a relationship together the way your normal, you know, son and father have. I feel bad the way he walks around with his head down all the time, always being ashamed, whatever happened in the past. Maybe I wanted to be like my father. . . . Some of the things I have done I am ashamed of, don't understand, but hell, maybe that had something to do with it. . . . You see, he wasn't a man after that moment. I don't know what you'd call it, he let Mom run . . . rule the roost. I think he just gave up. I said when I got on my own, a woman wouldn't run me."

Although he'd try to run away from home when he was a teenager, he finally had had enough when he was seventeen and physically challenged his father. When he won, life in the house was no longer possible. "When I was seventeen and we were sitting at the supper table and they started into an argument and I just couldn't take it no longer, why, I did it. My mother threw a cup of coffee or an ashtray at my father and my father threw coffee or something at my mother and I just jumped up and decked my father and my mother jumped up and smacked me and said 'Don't get between us no more,' and that was it. It was time for me to leave."

Shawcross was born in Kittery, Maine, but the family moved to New York when he was only a few months old. His father built the house himself on land given to him by his parents in an area immediately outside of Watertown, New York. Art's father's parents and his brothers lived just down the road. The whole family lived only hundreds of feet from one another in a part of the town people called "Shawcross Corners." At first the family home was very small, Art remembers, and didn't even have an indoor bathroom, but the father built more bedrooms and an indoor bathroom, adding on to the structure year after year as the family grew. At first all the children slept in the same room. Then the father separated the brothers and the sisters.

As a child growing up, he was beaten by both parents for real or imagined infractions. The beatings grew worse, he said, after his parents' fight over the letter from the unnamed woman. His mother would hit him across the back and his buttocks with a broom handle made from a green piece of wood. She would also hit him with a belt, he said. His father, he says, would chase him around the yard with a belt, sometimes getting so mad at him that he would forget which end of the belt he was using and draw blood when the buckle dug into Art's back. Thus, he told the court-appointed psychiatrist for the prosecution, he grew up in a household where physical beatings were a common experience.

Arthur also experienced severe head injuries during his childhood. Once, when he was still a little kid, shortly after his mother had received the letter about his father's previous marriage, he was taking part in what he called a "family feud." His cousins from Shawcross Corners were fighting with a group of children from a neighboring section when Art was hit over the head with a stone. He received a concussion, a bump that he says he still has, and it took a number of stitches to close the severe wound, but he doesn't recall any subsequent adverse effects other than childhood paralysis in his legs. He said that on a number of occasions after getting hit with the stone, he would be sitting in a chair and be unable to get to his feet because it was as if he had no feeling below his waist. He remembers that the feelings of paralysis almost caused him to drown in Lake Ontario once when he couldn't move his legs and began to sink below the surface of the water. His father pulled him out by his hair and, Shawcross says, saved his life.

When he was in high school and throwing the discus as a member of the track team, he was hit with a discus thrown errantly by another athlete on an adjoining range. The discus hit Shawcross in the front of the head, knocked him unconscious for many hours, and left him with a loss of memory of the entire incident. He awoke in the hospital and was disoriented for a long period of time after that.

In a subsequent accident, he was working as a member of a construction crew breaking rocks when he was told by the crew chiefs to hold one of the large rocks while a person wielding a sledgehammer tried to break it. Shawcross even told the prosecution psychiatrist that he wasn't having good feelings about it but held the rock as far away from him as he could while the man with the sledgehammer brought it squarely down—upon the side of Art's head. To this day he remembers very little about the incident except the way he felt when he was holding the rock far away from him. He felt no pain at the time, he said. Actually he felt nothing at the time because he didn't wake up until he had been in the hospital for many hours. He remembers that he was disoriented for a long period after that.

His final major head injury also occurred while he was working on a crew, this time while teetering precariously on the top rung of a forty-foot ladder, trying to pitch a large tent. It happened at Fort Benning, Georgia, after he had been drafted and had completed infantry training. As he reached to control the roof portion of the tarp, a gust of wind blew the tarp away from him and lifted the ladder off the ground. It fell over and he landed on the back of his head, also receiving a concussion. Shawcross was unconscious again but remembers that he awoke before the ambulance arrived and remembers the ride to the hospital. Shawcross received these three major head injuries before he was eighteen, was drafted, and went into the Army, where he was eventually given a tour of duty in Vietnam.

The head injuries he received and the rupture in his family that tore apart the fabric of his home life, humiliated his father, and diminished his respect for his own masculinity might have severely reduced his resiliency and his abilities to cope with

186

the early experiences he had with sex. When Shawcross told medical investigators and the prosecution psychiatrist his story of his aunt's sodomizing him—something his aunt has consistently denied—he did it with a kind of a numbness that was chilling. It seemed to have been "no big deal" to him. It happened, it made him uncomfortable at the time, it created a problem in the Shawcross home, and that was it. However, the invasiveness of the act (or his perception of the act) may well have been one of the precipitating incidents that created a hair-trigger sensitive response where sexual arousal was concerned.

As Shawcross described the incident, "When I was about eight, nine years old, my mother's sister visited us and when Dad wasn't around the house she'd walk around in her underwear all the time. She was in her twenties. . . . One day Mom wasn't there and I think that I had a problem with my legs at the time and I was playing on the kitchen floor and Tina's looking out the window or something, at the sink, and she got nothing on but bra and panties. And she just took me in the other room, sitting on the couch, and she started playing with me and having me play with her. That's how I learned about oral sex."

Shawcross said that she performed oral sex on him and had him perform oral sex on her. He does not remember whether he got an erection or whether he had an orgasm. He does not even remember whether it was pleasant or not. He only remembers that it stimulated levels of sexual arousal in him and the need for sexual excitation that carried over in his life well after his aunt had left. "I was scared at first, but then it didn't bother me after that. Only thing that bothered me is when she left and went home, I was wondering . . . right after that I started doing it with my sister."

As he describes it, he himself might not have felt humiliated at the time, but there were levels of shame associated with the act because he says that his mother found out about it and made his aunt leave.

"I think it was three, four days, five days later, I think, I think my mother found out, something that Tina said or something somewhere. They had an argument and Tina went back home."

He also said that he was aroused to the point of becoming fascinated with masturbation. "I was very upset when my aunt went back home. . . . After that I would play with myself, either in bed at night or in the bathroom, or outside in the woods near home."

Shawcross usually got in trouble for masturbating. He told the psychiatrist that after he had experienced paralysis in his legs, his aunt taught him how to give and receive oral sex, at which point he became so aroused that he was constantly masturbating. His mother became worried, he said, and began threatening him every time she thought he

188

was masturbating. When she caught him, he says, "She would run in with a butcher knife or something and grab a hold of me and scream and holler. . . . She had a paring or knife or a butcher knife in her hand and she'd show up in there." He says that his brother often told his mother he was masturbating and that would bring her into his room. "Sometimes I'd be on the top bunk and Jimmy on the bottom and the bed would move, wiggle, and Jimmy would holler, 'Mom, he's doing it again,' and she'd come running there and grab me and she said, 'I'll cut it off.' "

Shawcross was about ten at the time. It was the same year that he and a friend of his first began a sexual relationship. It happened, Shawcross told the court-appointed psychiatrist for the prosecution, after he almost drowned in a swamp he had fallen into. Shawcross had never learned to swim.

"I fell in the swamp, down maybe a quarter mile from the house. And I'm hollering, screaming down there, and this kid shows up—that was Michael, and he's a year younger than me and he was living in an old schoolhouse." Shawcross was afraid for his life, he told the doctors. "I was up to my neck in muck. All I could do was cry." Michael pulled Shawcross to safety and they went to a nearby creek to "soak the muck off and then walked around to dry off." They stopped in a pasture near a patch of woods and Shawcross took his clothes off and hung them on a clump of brush to dry them off. Then he soaked in a nearby stream to wash himself off further.

"Mike took his clothes off and jumped in also," Shawcross wrote. "After a while we were sunning ourselves off and I started to jack off. No reason, just did it. Mike did too. Then we would touch each other and then we did oral sex. That was my first experience with that. Mike and I got to be good friends.· Once in a while we would have our touching sessions. . . . One time at a farm nearby, about one and a half miles away, Mike and I started playing with sheep. We didn't know that sheep had organs like a woman. it felt good at the time."

Shawcross said that the man who owned the farm with his family first introduced him and his friend Michael to sheep. "We had this neighbor . . . he'd take us out to the barn. He had about thirty, forty sheep out there and he'd tell us, he says 'A single man can't own sheep,' and he'd have a sheep in the pen and he'd be cutting off all the wool and he'd cut the tail off the sheep and he'd put this white powder stuff on it and he'd show us. He says 'You see that? That's what a woman looks like.' "

When he was fourteen, Shawcross told psychiatrists, he began having sex with his sister, Jeanne, his cousin Linda, and a younger girl who lived down the road from Shawcross Corners. Art said that he used to give his sister oral sex when all the brothers and sisters slept in the same room on bunk beds and when the family used to go to the drive-in movies.

"My brother and I was sleeping on the top bunk and Donna and Jeannie had to be in the bottom bunk. And during the night I'd climb into their bed—and Jeannie always slept near the wall—and I'd get in there next to Jeannie. And sometimes when we'd go to drive-in movies I'd do the same thing with my cousin Linda. Linda was twelve, thirteen years old, a year older than Jeannie. . . . I was fourteen."

Shawcross says that he would be in the backseat with his sister and his cousin and he would perform oral sex on them while the rest of the family was watching the movie. He didn't have intercourse with them, he said, and they didn't perform oral sex on him. Shawcross says that he didn't feel guilty about it and, in fact, often fantasized about his sister when he masturbated after he was sent to prison. Shawcross also says that Jeannie was loyal to him during the entire period they were having sex. He thinks she liked it because he said she never complained to their mother about it. It all came about, he claims, because he had become aroused sexually by his aunt.

"I was troubled after Tina left. She gave me something, a new experience I didn't know anything about. I seemed to enjoy it. I had nowhere to turn to, and I turned to my sister Jeannie."

191

At about the same time that Shawcross was a young teenager, he also had a sexual relationship with a young girl who lived down the road from where the school bus picked him up each morning. But the relationship turned violent, Shawcross says, when her brother found out about them and demanded that Shawcross have sex with him, too.

"I was having oral sex with her and he caught me one day with her out behind the garage and he tells me if I didn't do the same thing for him he'd tell everybody. So I was forced to do him." Shawcross told the psychiatrist that he performed oral sex on the boy that one time. However, he said, "Another time he come at me and I went after him with a two-by-four . . . he never bothered me after that, and then I quit fooling around with his sister."

Art told his defense team that he became sexually crazed when he was fourteen and received pleasure from oral sex until he was raped by an older man.

"When I was fourteen, one night I stayed after school for wrestling practice and then I got off the school bus in Brownville, New York. It's only two miles. I was within a mile from home when a man in a red car, convertible, stopped to give me a lift. I didn't think about it. Just got in. Then he grabbed me by the throat and told me to take my pants down. I did. Then he held onto my balls and sucked me off. I was scared and crying, then the guy got mad because I couldn't come. He raped me. I was let off near home. I couldn't tell anyone what happened, either. After that, when I masturbated, I could not come until I inserted a finger in my ass. Why, I don't know!"

Shawcross says that his sexual experiences became increasingly violent as he became angrier and angrier after the rape. The residual rage that he felt touched raw nerves, according to his accounts of what happened that had first been exposed by his aunt. As Shawcross describes it, he learned to associate shame with the pleasure of sex, tried to satisfy his obsession with sex with himself — for which he was threatened with physical castration and mutilation by his mother — and later with his sister. He tried to satisfy himself in one voluntary homosexual relationship with one of his friends; he was forced to perform oral sex on another boy after he was found having oral sex with the boy's sister; and then he was violently raped by an older man who was choking him at the time. At the very least, the last of these incidents is enough to trigger a long-term post-traumatic stress-like disorder that could well remain active unless steps were taken to provide a remedy. Shawcross's assertion that he couldn't come and had to inflict pain on himself to achieve any satisfaction, if true, is especially revealing.

He turned his obsession with sex toward animals, he told the medical investigators. "One day I did it to a chicken; it died. Then a cow, dog, and a horse. I didn't know where this was leading up to. When I was seventeen I had sex with a girl that lived near us, only oral sex. She wouldn't do the other. Then I went and did the same thing with another girl nearby who lived on a farm. I got to like going down on girls. When I was eighteen I had sex with a girl of twenty-seven where I worked at the Watertown Bowling Alley. She was a waitress there at the bar. I learned everything that night."

Shawcross was also learning how to break into buildings and local private homes and running away from his own family with increasing frequency. His first burglary was at a local Sears retail store when he was about fifteen. "I didn't have no money for Christmas or anything. . . . I was seeing everybody else enjoying themselves and I had nothing and I was in Watertown and it was a stormy night with twenty-, thirty-foot icicles hanging on the side of a building, Sears and Roebuck, right outside the store. There was a traffic light there. Tractor trailers, they come up and they downshift at the light, making all kinds of noises before they get started, and I just hit one of those icicles and it fell in through the plate glass window and I just walked in. . . . The tractor trailers made so much racket shifting just to get moving no one heard the glass break."

Shawcross thought that he was safe in the store, but he didn't realize there was a burglar alarm as

194

well. "After I got in there, all these cash registers sitting there with the drawers open, nothing in them but pennies. I walked around downstairs and didn't touch nothing. I just walked around. Went upstairs, went up on the third floor, went in the main office, and they got these big double closet big metal cabinets. I open up the cabinet. There's all kinds of money in the cabinet right there in front of me and the bell started ringing. They got a big walk-in safe and all the money was in the cabinet.

"I ran downstairs and hid by the elevator, so when they finally caught me they give me probation because I didn't take nothing."

That was the first crime that became a part of Shawcross's record, even though prior to that break-in, when he was only thirteen, he had been breaking and entering private homes and hunting lodges in the area. He and his friend Michael—the boy he'd been having oral sex with—learned how to enter houses where the owners were away for extended periods of time. "Me and my friend Michael, we climbed up on the back of this one house, nobody was there, and up on the shed and up on the roof, went through the second story of the house, and went downstairs in the dining room or the living room. . . . We took a .22, a couple boxes of shells, went way down in the woods, and we were shooting at crows and things. At the end of the day, we were going to bring the gun back,

195

put it back where we found it. When we got back in the house we had a surprise. While we were down in the woods, somebody backed the truck up to the plate-glass picture window. They took everything, right down to the sink out of the wall. Somebody ripped the house off, so what's the sense of putting the gun back onto an empty shelf. People that owned the place was in Florida."

Shawcross and Michael performed other burglaries on empty houses in the area. They would enter houses with broken windows, look around, and find that most of the valuables had already been stolen. He also robbed a gas station without getting caught. "I worked at a gas station for a while. I used to take some money out of the till."

He remembered other times when he would leave home for a day, break into summer cottages in the area to steal food, clean up after himself, and leave. When he was fourteen, he ran away from home, hid at the zoo in Watertown, and broke into a local restaurant. "I was sitting up behind this place and the smell just started driving you crazy. You're hungry and starving and I would go down and look in the garbage cans, see if there was anything to eat there. And there was nothing there and this truck started pulling in and I ran and hid in some tall grass and I was sitting there watching. This guy goes to open the door and he fell out of the truck. He was drunk. He pulls up by the back door of the building. He unlocks the door and slides the door to the side and he's got an elevator on the back of the truck and he gets all this stuff out and—goes in the building. He stacks these boxes up in there, comes out and he slams the door, and he locks the lock, drives away. While he was in there putting stuff away, a cop car came in. Just seen him loading stuff into the building and he left. I'm sitting there with a watch, want to see what time the cop comes back. Was twenty-two minutes by the watch before the cop came around again. So I walk down there and—this guy, when he closed the lock, didn't lock the door. The door is still open. So I slid open the door. I slid the door closed. Now if you look from the front of the building, all the lights are on. You can see anybody walking around. . . . They got a shopping cart. I take a big fillet of haddock . . . baked beans . . . salads. Load up the shopping cart. Under the shelf they had cash containers full of change. I fill up my pocket with change and another pocket with bills."

After robbing the restaurant and finding food and money, Shawcross was able to live away from home in the zoo park on his own. "I stayed in the park for a week, built a fire, and grilled and stayed up there." Then, he said, he took the bus to Rochester, stayed there on the money he'd robbed, took another bus to Buffalo, where "a gun went off and I heard the ricochet on a building somewhere and I just turned around and got back on the bus and went to Syracuse. Ended up back at Watertown. They never asked me where I was, what I do." He was fourteen, by his own account, and had been gone for four weeks.

He was establishing a pattern of taking long sojourns by himself, traveling either on highways or backroads, extended stays in the woods, hiding in public parks, or simply hiding out in his own neighborhood, as an escape from what was going on in his family. He revealed that he had started running away from home and heading for the Canadian border when he was as young as ten or eleven, in the years immediately following his sexual encounters with his aunt and with his friend Michael.

Shawcross told psychiatrists that he was never able to smoke or drink before he went to Vietnam. He said that he had such an adverse reaction to beer, for example, that even the smell of it would make him sick. It was the same with cigarettes, he said, because the fumes would make him nauseous. He told one story to the prosecution psychiatrist about the time he had gone into a bar in Brownville, New York, about two or so miles out of Watertown. "I think I had eleven dollars in my pocket when I went in. Got a beer. I was sitting there and don't remember what happened, but I came home with eleven dollars in one pocket and over a hundred dollars in another pocket. So I went back the next day and I think my father went in the bar, talked to the guy, and he says, 'Where did he get all the money?' and he says, 'He didn't miss one pool shot.' I was shooting pool and the fumes of the place got me drunk. I don't even think I had a sip of beer, just sitting there playing pool and just the fumes. For a long time, years after, I wouldn't touch no alcohol."

It's not farfetched that Shawcross has an allergic reaction to alcohol that's intense enough to cause mental blackouts, especially if there is any history of alcoholism on either side of his family. Some adult children of alcoholics, for example, rather than being alcoholics themselves, have intense physical counterreactions to alcohol, as if their systems are allergic to the chemicals. Many can't drink wine or beer because it causes such violent reactions or causes blackouts. Shawcross's story, if true, is not at all improbable.

Shawcross said that he got married for the first time when he was nineteen. "We got married in 1964. We had a baby on October 2, 1964. Everything was okay for a while, then I started doing strange things again. I'd pick up girls near where we lived in Sandy Creek, New York. We had sex. Sometimes with others as well. I couldn't stop myself. Just the desire to have more."

His first wife was Sarah Chatterton, a local girl who was a year older than he. Together they had a child who told reporters for the Rochester newspapers after his father was arrested that he worried he carried some of the same genetic markers that caused his father to commit crimes throughout his life.

Relations with Sarah — Arthur called her Sally — soured almost immediately after they were married, because of her father. "I was in love with Sally, but things started getting bad when we started moving, living right next to her mother and father."

They divorced after he got drafted and went into the Army. Shawcross said he made the guy who wanted to marry Sarah buy him out of the marriage, which he didn't care for anyway. For him, it was purely a business transaction, because Sarah's fiancé was so desperate to go to Mexico, get the divorce papers finalized, and marry Sarah.

By 1968 Shawcross was divorced and only months away from his tour of duty in Vietnam. From that point on, he told psychiatrists, his entire life changed dramatically for the worse. He would become a walking time bomb.

Chapter 11
"The Ghost of the Jungle"

Shawcross claims that his years in South Vietnam were his crucible. Not only did he manage to stay alive in Vietnam while he could see American soldiers dying all around him, he said he was transformed by his tour of duty. Even in the moments just before his confession to the Genesee River murders, his wife, Rose, told him that it was Vietnam that turned him into a monster. In the biography he wrote for his medical investigators, he said that he saw himself turning into a monster as he killed more and more people.

Shawcross was already a troubled youth when he was shipped in-country. He had gone AWOL in the United States once because of a mixup in his orders and in receiving his pay allotment, but he managed to talk his way out of serving any time. When he received orders to be stationed in Germany for the duration of the war—every soldier's dream from 1965 to 1975—he said he told his company commander that either he was going to Vietnam or he was going to Canada: it was the Army's choice. He said that before he shipped out the Army gave him a twenty-three day leave to clear up his affairs. Art told his parents and friends that he did not expect to return from the war.

With his divorce final and with the money he made from Sarah's fiancé, he returned home to party with friends and see a girl he was dating named Linda Neary. He told her, three days before he had to report for duty, that he wanted to get married. "I says, 'I don't love you, but I don't know if I am coming back, so you would have an allotment.' " That was his proposal. Her family had enough money, he contended that she didn't need an Army "surviving heir" allotment, but it was his way of saying that he wanted to be family.

They got married so quickly, in a town named Mexico, New York, that Linda didn't even tell her parents. She made Art wait in one of the cottages on her parents' property until she told her father, and then they came out and got him. His marriage to Linda was so ephemeral that when he eventually did get back from Vietnam, his parents had to remind him that not only was he married, but that the Army had been sending his paychecks to his wife for the past thirteen months. It all came as a complete shock to him, he said, when he remembered it. It came as an even bigger shock when his wife told him that she had used his money to buy her father presents because she thought the money was hers.

Shawcross said he arrived a good nineteen days ahead of the troop ship where he was supposed to be billeted. It had left the day before Shawcross came to California, so the Army posted him to fly standby on a transport to Saigon, where he waited in the 93rd Placement Center as a cook until the troop convoy finally arrived. He joined his unit and was sent up-country to Pleiku in a C-130 transport.

At first, he told his psychiatrist, he was simply a supply clerk filling orders and making sure they got shipped out to the correct units. Then he was assigned to arrange for the transportation of ammunition. He said that he had a warrant officer assigned to him who would transport him to any firebase in the Central Highlands to make sure that all the weapons shipped out from our supply office got to the bases. "I wanted to go wherever our companies were. So I go out to all these firebases for a while. I would land and go to the CP and I would tell them who I am and I have my clipboard and I would have a little booklet with the clipboard of what battalion is there and I would know what he's got. I would go through trying to figure out, check everybody's weapon. I couldn't do it. They would get men before I get there and they would come in there with weapons

203

I don't even have on my roster. I just do the best I could."

Shawcross said he became adept at modifying weapons for special purposes such as hunting. "Over there they had this thing where by Geneva Convention you couldn't have silencers, couldn't have shotguns. Everybody had shotguns, had twelve-gauge sawed-off, everything, ten-gauge. I would take baby bottle nipples and I would stretch them over the M-16 with a nightscope and I would shoot monkeys out of a tree or we would shoot rats in front of the bunker line. The nipples would suppress great. You couldn't hear nothing. No report. Nothing, 'Poo,' just like that! I would get nipples from the PX. When I couldn't get them from the PX, I had to order from the States."

Being able to suppress the sound of an M-16, Shawcross said, allowed him to kill in the woods and not be heard. The nipples were so effective, they even fit over the flash suppressor and effectively camouflaged the entire weapon. With the silencer and a nightscope, Shawcross was more of an assassin than a soldier, and he used it effectively after he went off on his own for days at a time to roam the jungles after his near emotional collapse at seeing American soldiers getting killed by hostile fire for the first time. It was an emotion trauma for Shawcross, he says, and it forever changed him. It made him into a killer, he told the court-appointed psychiatrist.

It happened ten miles west of Kontum at a firebase known as Superstition Mountain near the Ho Chi Minh Trail. "When I was up there, I seen guys getting dropped, shot up. And I started smoking at that moment and I just cried and didn't know what to do. I was scared, ducked down, and I am sitting there with four machine guns, M-60's. I'm on a hill firebase out in the jungle. . . . I had never fired them before. Don't know how they fired or anything. They just supplied up from Saigon and brought up and sent up two of our trucks and took them to the firebase. . . . Something was across the valley on another hillside and something was shooting at us. We could see the smoke and guys dropping like flies all over the place. And I just quick hooked everything up and just started shooting and bullets going everywhere but where I wanted them to go. I changed everything all up and finally got everything going. One guy goes down into the jungle, starts shooting uphill, and something blew up over there and we ran. . . . They found a few bodies over there and seventy-five recoilers and maybe a gun over there, and I couldn't take it. I just got on the chopper when it came back in and went back to Kontum. I am just sitting there on the bunk: smoke, smoke, smoke. And the sergeant comes in the tent. He tells me, he says, 'You know, everybody goes through that. Some worse than others. Some don't make it.' "

For someone like Shawcross who didn't live by the rules, Vietnam, for all its horror and blood, became more like a game than a war. Shawcross was reckless; he didn't believe in following orders, and he said he wasn't afraid to take risks. But he was terrorized by the place and shocked by the violence until he decided to become more violent than the war. That was when—if we take his story as a gloss on reality, if not reality itself—the traumas he experienced in Vietnam numbed him to the feeling, empathy, and pain that are a part of the course of normal human existence.

First, Shawcross explained to us in his journal that he kept lead-lined connex boxes in his tent during periods of 100-degree-plus heat. He says that he even slept in an ammunition box. When we ran toxicological tests on Shawcross after his arrest, we found that his serum lead levels were higher than average. We found that his system had been contaminated by lead poisoning. One of the symptoms of lead poisoning is hallucinations and an inability to mediate between behavioral extremes. As Shawcross described his experiences in Vietnam, he described an individual who may well have been reacting to lead poisoning.

Shawcross also says that he ate roasted animals and rice out of lead-lined boxes as well. Therefore he may have been directly ingesting lead as well as inhaling fumes. By the time he returned to the United States after his tour, his mental capacity might have been significantly diminished along with his capacity to moderate his behavior. His emotional resiliency, already weak, might have been diminished even further.

His stories of grandiosity and the great improbability of his exploits lend credence to his exhibiting some form of behavior disorder. Yet Shawcross also adds an element of plausibility to some of his stories. He makes them sound so illogically real — "It could only happen to me" — that you might even tend to believe him despite the incredible nature of it all.

Shawcross said that by February, 1968, he had experienced another change in his behavior after someone close to him was killed. "One of my men got hit in the face. Something happened to me then. I started to smoke, even to drink rice wine or smoke pot. Then, in May of '68 I was given R & R in Hawaii. I met my wife Linda there. We had a good week together, but I couldn't wait to get back to Nam! When I got back I would go off by myself and look for the enemy by myself."

At that point, he says, he began killing like a predator. He was no longer in the war, he was fighting the war all by himself on a personal level. Vietnam was where, if Shawcross's story is to be taken at face value, he *became* a serial killer, trolling for victims in the jungle. "I think at that moment I was beyond reality or something like that. I'd just walk in a daze. I went down into a valley and I seen a woman down there and I shot her and dragged her up on the side of a hill and she wasn't dead yet. I tied her to a tree where I made a little camp and she was putting an AK-47 in a tree. I went down. There was a big hollow tree. All kinds of rifles in there, ammunition there, and they had a little footpath going there, up into the woods. I went up in there and found a couple of huts up on stilts. And so I am standing there and they got a little ladder going into one and I hear somebody in there and I tap on the side of the hooch and a girl comes out. I tie her up and walk her back up and tied her to the tree next to that other girl inside the hut where they were living. Underneath the hut was all kinds of food, rice, ammunition. They're the enemy. I get up there and I cut one, I cut her throat. I took her head off. Sometimes Vietnamese are superstitious. I put her head on a pipe like a fence post where rifles are. I shoved it in the mud. I went back up there. I just wasn't me no more. I never done anything like that in my life. I took that woman's leg off from the hip to the knee—the ham section of the body—and roasted it on a fire. Didn't smell too good, but when about burnt, I began to eat some of it. Eating flesh cooked over a fire tasted like pork, like monkey. Took the body and put it on an ant-hill. While I'm sitting there cooking the one, the other girl watching me passes out and is peeing on herself. Then I raped her but first I gave her oral sex. She couldn't understand what I was doing, but her body did. I untied her, then retied her to two other small trees. Afterward I ate some more, then sat sharpening my knife and watching her. She fainted several times. I cut her slightly from her neck to her crotch. She screamed and shit herself. I took out my M-16, pulled on a nipple, then put the gun to her forehead and pulled the trigger. Finally I cut her head off and put it on another stick where the house was. It was where the NVA got water. I took that girl, I just strung her up by her feet and butchered her just like I would a cow. Why? A few days later I told some guys I met on a trail to go there and get the guns and ammo. They burned everything but left the heads alone. The NVA never went back to those spots. Superstition. The NVA tortured us, why couldn't we torture them?"

Shawcross said that when he killed, he used a baby nipple over the muzzle of his M-16 to suppress the crack of the rifle. He could kill at a distance with one silent shot which he called a "poo." Soon he was going off on patrol by himself. "Some days I'd be out two or three days at a time. No one asked me where I was. I killed the enemy as I found them. All had weapons. Most of them didn't hear the shot that hit them. I was a ghost in the jungle . . . one bullet and no sound."

Shawcross says that he killed children in Vietnam because the VC used to chain children to trees where they could fire down on American patrols as they made their way through the jungle. "Somebody in a tree shot and one of our men fell and I had a machine gun and I shot up into the tree. Other guys were shooting, too. We shot where the smoke was. Then we had to cut the tree down and find there was a young kid chained to the tree with one round. I felt bad."

Shawcross said that they couldn't see the sniper who had shot at them so they simply fired at where the shot came from. The sniper didn't fall, because he was actually chained into the tree firing an M-1 that was wired to the tree limbs. The M-1 had one round in it, Shawcross said. The kid was supposed to die. It might have all been part of a strategy to get the American soldiers to shoot Vietnamese children to so dehumanize them that they would become useless as disciplined soldiers.

As the stress of the war and the killing affected him more and more, Shawcross said that he would take longer and longer solitary patrols into the jungle. The American war machine was breaking down in Vietnam, he wrote. More and more soldiers were committing acts of individual terrorism or heroism, depending upon how you looked at it, as the discipline at the firebases and jungle outposts began to deteriorate. Shawcross began killing for the thrill of it and for the sake of striking terror into the Vietnamese whenever he could. He said that he could get into the jungle, track enemy troops, bring them down silently, and sneak away. He took pride in striking out of the darkness, he said, and at times described the experience as "beautiful."

"I was all by myself everyday. Sometimes I took a radio and just went out in the woods and sit three, four days, mostly watching, hoping somebody would come by. Another time when I walked from Kontum to the firebase Dak To I came upon a small pond in the little valley near dark. I found a spot to hide in for the night. When it was full dark, I crawled down to the water with a canteen to refill. As I was laying there, I felt a vibration in the ground. I froze and moved real slow to the water. I found that water warmer than usual. That pond was a fake, far under the water was some kind of tarp. I took the water anyway and went back to the hiding spot and looked around. I was scared, but excited also. I did not find an entrance so I moved around the hills, slowly as not to get caught.

On the western side deep in the jungle I found a dirt road. Well worn, too. So I found a sort of cave to watch plus keep out of sight. I had at least fifty bottle nipples with me. Near morning the vibrations in the ground stopped and people started walking up that small road to the west toward Laos. No noise or talking. Too many of them to shoot. So I followed them as best I could. Most kept that road in sight. About mid-afternoon I seen smoke coming up out of the jungle about three to four miles from where I was on top of a good-sized hill. Never once did I find a trail. I knew what was out there and at night I knew also what I was going to do. Scare them! Make them think of the ghost.

I found my first spot with a clear sight on a small fire. Five people were sitting and eating and drinking. Lots of noise, too. One guy had a cup in his hand, shot it right out of his hand. No one moved. That guy started to cry. These people look up at the sky and cry. He still had the handle in his hand. . . . They can understand getting shot at, but not to hear a gun going off does something to the mind. That camp was a riot. Then I started to shoot people at random. Mostly head shots. I always left a nipple on a bush. I shot twenty-six people that night."

As Shawcross wrote in his journal and described the incidents of the war to the psychiatrists, he became more haunted. He described fewer and fewer of his own exploits and dwelled more on the terrorizing and dehumanizing aspects

212

of his tour of duty. He described not only what the Vietnamese did to the Americans or what the Americans did to the Vietnamese, but what the Vietnamese or the Koreans did to each other. These stories may all be fantasies — veterans' organizations have not confirmed them and we have not found any independent corroboration of them — but Shawcross said that he believed them to be true. If he believed them, his actions after the war were based on them, and they have to be taken seriously whether or not they are fantasies. In his own words, he described himself turning into a ghoul. "I was a mean bastard, too. I was like hot and cold water, on and off at will. I could turn something aside at will and forget. I can't hide the fact that something was wrong with me. I ate human flesh over there. Same thing I did here. I couldn't help it. The urge was too strong. I was becoming a monster of sorts."

The memories of the war torment him to this very day. "Vietnam was a haunting experience in my life. Girls over there were whores from the age of nine to fifteen. I had a girl named Froggy in Dak To who was eleven; Kie in Pleiku was thirteen, Lyn in Kontum was twenty-four. One South Vietnamese soldier found an old woman selling Coke. Never buy Coke in a bottle. They made her drink one of the six bottles she had. She died on the spot. Battery acid! Came right out her stomach. I remember one time in Pleiku

213

a small little girl about six walked into a bunch of GIs and exploded. Another time there was a fat little girl sitting on a pile of dirt and she was not moving. We did not get close but walked around her. Good thing, too. She had a wire around her waist going down the crack of her ass into the ground. We had a jeep with us. Put a loop under her arms and a good hundred feet of rope between her and the jeep. That jeep and that girl came off that pile in two ways: pulled and pushed. She left a thirty-foot crater. Lost one foot also.

"I went into a village in Kontum and they had a whorehouse in there. And the sergeant major come running out of a building holding himself, blood all over the place. A girl had a cup inside her with a razor blade in it and he split himself like a banana. So they took the girl and they tied her legs to a tree. And he took her clothes off and a ROK Korean that was with us—we had thirty of them in the battalion and these guys, you know, they didn't care for nothing—he took a machete and cut her from her asshole to her bellybutton. They just split her. And they tried to talk to her and she's spitting at everybody, cursing everybody out and they just cut her open and poo, split her right open."

If these stories are true, then it's not farfetched that most of Shawcross's behavior toward the prostitutes he was seeing in Rochester might have been determined by what he saw soldiers do to the prostitutes in Vietnam. The incidents were so vivid and violent that it would be hard to suppress the feelings associated with them. The GIs' behavior toward the prostitutes was motivated by revenge and by a deep hatred for being in a country where they themselves were targeted by people they believed to be the local population and for whom they were supposed to be fighting. Nothing made sense except the violence and the release of sexual tensions associated with that violence.

Chapter 12
Stateside

Shawcross left Vietnam as quickly and as effortlessly as he'd entered it. Only nobody bothered to find out how he was feeling when he was shipped back. "I was out in the jungle every day to about maybe thirty days before I left Vietnam. I just couldn't stay on base camp. Then, when I came back to the States, they had no debriefing or nothing. You just go back from the war zone. You are home. You are back in the States that quick."

He complained that he would have rather stayed in Vietnam because he was achieving a measure of accomplishment for the first time in his life: he was winning the war; he was killing the enemy wherever he found him. "I wasn't ready for the States, I was too keyed up, too hyper. I should have stayed another six months. I left Vietnam and flew to Japan, then to Alaska, then to Washington State. Stayed there for twenty-four hours, then flew to Chicago. Stayed at the airport four hours, then got a ride in a private Lear jet to Detroit, then to Syracuse. I was taken to the bus station in Syracuse. Stayed overnight. The next morning people started calling me names, baby killer. If I had a gun. . . ."

From Syracuse, Shawcross caught the bus to Watertown and went straight to see his mother. His arm was still bandaged from a recent bullet wound, and his jacket sleeve was pinned back over his bandaged arm. He'd thought nothing of it. "Got to Watertown about one P.M. and went up the street where my mother worked. Went and asked the girl if I could see Mrs. Arthur Shawcross. She said no. I went up by her and into the manager's office. Held the door shut. Told the guy what I wanted and where I came from. He got up fast enough. Took me into the warehouse where lots of people were working. My mom passed out when she seen me. Everyone else started crying. My left sleeve was pinned up like I had one arm. Left there and we all went home."

Without any decompression period, he was back in the house and the war was supposed to be over. But for Shawcross the real war was just beginning. "I was still hyper and I couldn't stop talking. Once mom slapped my face by my saying, 'Dinks.' That's the name we had for the VC. But she took it another way. I got up from the table, went into the living room. Sat on the couch for a while. Then I went outside. I was mad. Couldn't control my emotions."

Shawcross's experience was an example of one of

the typical problems experienced by most veterans when they returned home from the war zone. They had spent nine to twelve months in emotionally charged, highly stressful, and horror-filled situations. Yet when they got back to the states, little if anything had changed in the world around them. The war was not a shared experience, the way World War Two had been shared by an entire country. Veterans were expected to slip back into their lives as easily as slipping back into civilian clothes and closing a door on their battlefield experiences. There was no way to shed load and very few people understood what post-traumatic stress was. As a result, many veterans never worked through the problems they had in integrating the violence of the war into their lives. Shawcross was one of these casualties of war. This doesn't justify in any way what he did, but it helps explain why the events he says he experienced accelerated his decline into violence. If Shawcross exaggerated his experiences to make them worse, it shows that he needed that violence to explain to himself why he was racked by feelings of rage.

Clearly, however, when Shawcross came home from the war, he was as alone as he had ever been in his life. He was so totally absorbed in his own feelings that he had blocked out the events that immediately preceded his leaving for Vietnam. He told psychiatrists that he stayed in his house for a full three days before his mother asked him if he had any plans to see his wife.

"My mother says, 'Ain't you going to see Linda?' I said 'Linda who?' I forgot I was married. So I took my bags and was driven up Route 12. Stuck up my thumb and got a ride right away. When I got to Clayton, I ask if we could stop at the bank. I had $2000 in there, I thought. The bank told me I had $3.48 left. I walked out in a daze. I was driven to our driveway and let off. I tried to carry my bags, but couldn't with one arm. So I left everything at their trailer and walked up to the house. Linda and some guy were sitting on a chair in the front yard. I seen them but they did not see me. The house was built on top of the garage, so I went into the garage door, up the stairway, and knocked at the door. My father-in-law opened the door, seen me, and hollered for Lois, his wife. She went out the front door and got Linda. By the time I got to the door, that guy was gone. First my mom upset me and then Linda and the bank account. I just sat on the deck for a few hours. What could I do? I felt strange. The quiet scared me."

Shawcross—the kid who said he was emotionally and sexually abused as a child and raped by an older man when he was a teenager; the boy who tried to run away from home on numerous occasions and who was already breaking into other people's property; the soldier who said that he murdered women and children, mutilated and tor-

219

tured them, and devoured their flesh—is finally home. Within seventy-two hours after his arrival in Watertown, his mother has slapped him and humiliated him, sending him back outside to stew in his own fury; she reminds him that he is supposed to be married; he finds that his bank account, which he thought he had built up during his tour of duty, is empty; and then he discovers his wife entertaining another man in her apartment.

Shawcross was almost in shock, he says. And the nightmares about his experiences and his feelings started almost immediately. Before he realized it, homicidal feelings were coming to the surface and he was taking out his rage and frustration on his wife. Neither of them expected him to return from Vietnam. But he did. And that person who came home from the war was different—and far worse, by his own account, than the person who left.

Shawcross says that Linda Neary's family were Christian Scientists. They didn't smoke or drink. That was fine with him when he and Linda were first married, he explained, because he didn't smoke or drink either. However, after seeing GIs get killed for the first time in Vietnam, Shawcross began smoking heavily. When he got to Linda's house in Watertown—he and Linda were renting a cottage from her parents—he and his mother-in-law got into a fight over his smoking. "I was smoking like a fiend. My mother-in-law comes in and takes all the ashtrays out. She says, 'You can't have an

220

ashtray.' I said, 'I am paying fifty dollars a month rent here.' I says, 'Your ass stays right out there because what I do is my business.' Her father, if he wanted to have a cigarette, he had to go outside. If he wanted a beer he had to go downtown."

The first arguments, Shawcross said, began over money. "All right, I was in Vietnam, I was sending money home every month. I was making $150, $200, voluntarily taking patrols from other guys. I'd drive a truck from one firebase to another. Guys were scared. They just didn't want to go, and I didn't care. I just . . . just take the money and go, and I'd send it home. I get back to Clayton, when I got home, and I had a couple grand, around there, and she only got $3.48 in that account. I asked her, 'What happened to the money in the bank?' She said, 'Bought my father a boat for his birthday.' I says, 'You got money. I ain't got no money.' Her father retired from AT&T from New Jersey. He's got a phone in the house, one in the trailer, one in the car, and gets $25 for each telephone free a month. He's got stocks in AT&T, so they are not hurting. And she goes and spends all the money we got in our account. Had nothing to start with."

Shawcross still had five or six months to serve on his term of enlistment and had to return to Fort Sill, Oklahoma, where he was training recruits. At the same time, he explained, he had begun to have nightmares and visions of what he had done in

221

Vietnam. "The first few nights living with her while on leave, I was just fighting in my sleep. She's a blonde, blue-eyed girl and she'd be touching me and waking me. She tried to wake me up so I would stop fighting. I don't know but I beat on her when I was asleep. She looked like a raccoon the next morning—blonde girl with two black eyes. They wanted to have me arrested. They told a town cop and the cop told me, 'You get these feelings,' he says, 'go somewhere. Go out in the woods somewhere.' Even after I got out of the Army and went back to Clayton, Fourth of July that year, I never went around where they had any fireworks."

Shawcross and his wife were assigned to an apartment off-base while Arthur took over the arms room and helped set up ordinance exhibitions for military shows. While he was at Fort Sill, the nightmares and violence continued. Shawcross sought help from one of the psychiatrists on the base, but it was 1968 and the problems of returning Vietnam servicemen had not reached public awareness. The Army was still trying to figure out what was wrong with the GIs who complained of violent memories, terrifying visions, flashbacks, and nightmares. The psychiatrist, however, believed that Shawcross did have a problem, and after extensive interviews with Art, he recommended to Linda that Shawcross spend a period of time in a hospital for evaluation and treatment. He said that Shawcross might become violent because of what he said he had experienced in Vietnam.

Linda told investigators after Shawcross's arrest in Rochester that when she spoke to the Army psychiatrist at Fort Sill and he recommended that her husband be hospitalized, she was only about twenty years old and a Christian Scientist who did not believe in hospitals. Not only had she had very little experience with doctors and hospitals, she had been living with Shawcross as his wife for only a few months. She didn't even know the man and hadn't expected him to return from Vietnam alive. She said that when the doctor handed her the commitment papers, she was in no position to sign them. Linda Neary said that rather than fill out and sign the commitment papers, she had called Arthur's mother for advice. She said that she asked Bessie to fill out the papers, but Bessie said that it was her problem and refused to intervene. As a result, the Army had no reason to commit Shawcross to a mental hospital.

Shawcross himself said that he tried to talk to the Army doctor about what was bothering him but all he could do was sit there silently. He explained that he was so bottled up inside—there was so much anger, humiliation, and shame about what he had done in Vietnam and so much fear about how much he could be prosecuted for murder over there—that he simply didn't talk about it. Much of what he did, or what he fantasizes he did, eats away at him from the inside, he explains, like the battery acid in the Coke bottles that the Vietnamese soldier forced the old woman to drink.

"Maybe what bugs me is those two women I butchered. I lay here and wake up crying, Why? All these years I've tried to forget and it now haunts me. I break out with sores from my nervousness. . . . I keep trying to think of something to do with those two women. Maybe it will come out. There was something I may have been looking for in those prostitutes. But only June Stotts was not one. The woman I only knew as Jay. Why her? I got scared from what she said. Why? I want to know.

"That other girl in the jungle that I killed where I had taken off her head and placed it on a pole by a creek. I took her and butchered her like a steer, neck down. I had to use the machete and cut her on the body down the middle. Then cleaved the backbone and wash the blood out. Why? I wish I knew for sure. The same way you cut a deer I did to the body. Back in 1965 I had a job at the Adams Meat Market at Adams, New York. Just south of Watertown. This is where I learned to butcher nineteen cows and bulls a day. It was nothing new to me. Once the outside skin is taken off, who can tell? Yes, I did roast half the body, too, about the way a good well-done roast beef is cooked. Almost dry. The meat lasts for days that way. The rest of what I did not take I placed on a good-sized anthill. The ants will do the rest. Who could I talk to to understand what I am going through now because of all this? Twenty-three years of stored memories that are bothering me badly. The body of the other woman I placed on another ant mound. . . . I was a sick fool."

The Army psychiatrist back in 1969 said that he had finally had enough. He told Shawcross that he needed help but that without his cooperation the Army couldn't help him. A few months later Arthur and Linda packed up their bags, and immediately after his discharge they drove nineteen hours nonstop from Lawton to Pulaski, New York. "Right away after we got home," Shawcross said, "I started having problems with Linda."

Shawcross explained that one of the major problems had to do with his wife's family's belief in Christian Science. He revealed to doctors that it frightened him. He was most fearful of what he called the "magic" that had to do with the way Linda was once healed from what he described as a stomach tumor.

"When we was living in the cottage she had a bulge on her stomach. I took her to the doctors in Alexandria Bay, New York. Linda and her mother are Christian Science. They don't believe in medicine, makeup, doctors, or nothing—hospitals. So while I had a doctor examine her, mother comes in, grabs Linda, takes her out, and she starts hollering at me, 'What right do you got to take my daughter?' I says, 'She's my wife.' I thought she

225

was pregnant or something was wrong with her. Then we find out she had a tumor. So her and her mother pack up and they're gone for a week or two. I don't know where they went. When they came back, Linda was just like the day I met her. The bulge was gone, and I was scared. I said, 'Where did you go?' She says, 'When you join the church, we'll tell you.' I thought it was witchcraft, and I just went 'Bye, bye.' "

Shawcross remembered that Linda's family wouldn't let him leave at first. Every time he tried to run away, her father would do something to prevent him. He said he was scared and felt trapped by the world. There was nothing he could do to escape. Finally, he had to get the police to intervene, but even that didn't work.

"I had to leave and they had the car. Now, when I came to get the car, the car wouldn't start. Her father took the starter out. I go get the town cop. Cop comes up and says, 'You got to put the starter back in the car.' He puts the starter back in the car. So I came back the next day; it won't start. Somebody took the distributor cap. So every time I come over there, something was taken off the car so it won't start. So I took the cop over there and we stood there until they put everything back. Then I drove it away. Linda ended up with the car anyway. Took everything I had."

But getting out of the marriage wasn't easy for a person who when he was younger simply used to walk away from his problems. Even in Vietnam, Shawcross says, he used to go on solitary patrols whenever he was angry and take his feelings out on the VC or the peasants whose paths he crossed. Living with Linda Neary and her parents, however, was a different story. They had him trapped and were pushing him into a church that he felt was more magic than religion. He had to break out.

"I'm trying to get Linda away from her mother and she didn't want to go. I had a problem. I was mad at the world, and one night in a rainstorm I was walking to where I was staying, and I burnt a barn down. Why, I just burned it down. I just walked in, lit it, kept going. Then I get to the village of LaFargeville and I was working at Crowley's Cheese Company. I was making cottage cheese. I was one of the cooks and I was getting more aggravated there and I started a fire in there. I got picked up for that."

Shawcross also said that prior to setting the fire, he picked up two teenagers who were hitchhiking in the neighborhood. He says that he didn't know that they had broken into a gas station and that they had left their stolen goods in Shawcross's car. When the police searched for the stolen goods and found them in Shawcross's car, he was arrested and sent to jail on a possession of stolen goods charge. Nothing he could do would convince the police that he hadn't taken part in the robbery, he complained. To his mind, it was just one more grievance that he had against the world. To Linda's family, it was one more indicator that he was damaged goods and not a worthy husband for their child. They wanted Shawcross to leave and stay away from them after he was released from jail. That, Shawcross says, was what made him madder than anything else.

In his rage and in his inability to do anything about his problems, he says, he set the two fires that got him sent to the state penitentiary. He set the first fire at Knowltons Brothers Paper Mill on April 24, 1969. He set the second fire at Crowley's later in that year and was arrested in September for both fires. Shawcross confessed to the police that not only did he deliberately set the fire at Knowltons', he set it because he couldn't control his nervous anger at the world. He said that he had become aggravated at Crowley's just as he had at Knowltons Brothers. In both places he was unable to cope with outside pressures and he said he was reacting to having to work inside when he'd rather have been working on an outside job.

Shawcross's crime was particularly serious, especially for a person who had been through or who had imagined he had been through the violent sexual experiences he described. Fire is a form of sexual release for sexually dysfunctional individuals. Arson, therefore, is a violent example of that kind of dysfunction. It is not by chance that almost every serial killer whose life I have researched has been involved with fire-starting or has admitted to a fascination with fires. Fire-starting is one of the red flags that indicate a potential sexual offender in combination with other antisocial or aggressive acts. In Shawcross's situation, the two cases of arson were like large signposts marking his descent into homicidal madness and violent sexual crimes.

He was sentenced to five years at the state penitentiary at Attica, where he says he was raped by three black inmates. "Got raped in Attica by three black guys. I was lost, threatened, and in pain. I got all three my way, their way. I hurt them like they did me. I used a sock with soap as a black jack. Knocked them out and then screwed them and then smashed them once in the nuts. Was never bothered after that. I stayed in Attica about six months and then went to Auburn Prison."

After spending two years at Auburn, Shawcross says, he was caught in the 1971 race riots, but it became his ticket out of jail. "There was a riot in the center yard. The Black Panthers started hitting cops and guards right and left with whatever they had, taking their clubs. And I was standing next to an old man. He was sixty-something years old and he was bent over. What was he doing inside, anyway? A guy walks up to him with a sock with sand or something in it and he told the guy, he says, 'Give me your club,' and he says 'I can't give it to you.' And the guy hit him, took the club. Another guy comes over, hits him with a pipe, and laid it

229

open. The pipe was flat at one end. It laid open right in the head. The blood was squirting out of his head, but he didn't fall. His coat got hung up on the fence behind him. So they take off back down through the yard and I see this blood squirting out of him and I just reached up and put my finger on the pressure point and reached up behind and got his coat loose and half-dragged him all the way around the fence to the elevator. And the door opens up and I see these shotguns and the big state troopers and I told the guy, 'Put your thumb next to mine.' I said, 'You feel the pulse?' And he said, 'Yes.' I says, 'Don't remove it until the doctor tells you to.' A week later I went home."

The man whose life Shawcross had saved was a prison officer who was trying to disarm one of the rioters when he was clubbed. As a reward for saving the man, Shawcross was granted an accelerated parole and was sent back to Watertown, where he met his third wife. He had been divorced from Linda while he was in Attica, he said. She had come down to the prison with her mother and the divorce papers after Arthur had been sentenced and got him to sign them. He turned over what little property he had to her—she indicated that he would have very little use for it on the inside anyway—and by the time he was released, he was looking for another companion.

Now it was 1972. Arthur Shawcross was out of prison. He had not only not healed, he was even more angry and violent after having spent two and a half years on the inside of one of New York State's toughest penitentiaries. All the wounds from Vietnam had been reopened by the violence of the prison riot. And the deep scars which he said he carried because of the sexual abuse and rape he described as having experienced as a child had also been reopened by the rape he said he experienced at the hands of three Attica inmates. By the time he walked out the main gate of Auburn prison in 1971, Shawcross was a cauldron of rage, ready to attack whoever crossed him.

Tragically, the first people to cross him were two children.

Chapter 13
"I Buried Her Alive"

"Jackie Blake lived in the neighborhood," Shawcross said about the boy he was accused of killing in 1972. He knew him as one of the pack of kids who used to fish in the local ponds and streams. Shawcross knew most of the kids around the area and they knew him. The police knew him also. Shawcross had become a local fixture back in Watertown, where he returned after serving half of his five-year sentence for arson. He had gotten a job doing "whatever needed doing" for the Watertown Public Works Department and tried to settle into the routine of life once again. He'd even married a girl who he'd known for years and who had two children from a previous relationship. She hadn't seen Shawcross since the two of them had been children, but she wanted to get married. "I didn't want to shame my parents," she told a reporter for the *Rochester Democrat and Chronicle*. "I was a woman with two little kids, and I saw the opportunity to get a man to support them."

"I met a girl that went to school with my sister

Jeannie," Shawcross told his medical investigators. "Her name was Penny Nichol, and she lived over at the Cloverdale Apartments at that time." Shawcross said that what made her so attractive to him was not her smile, or her personality, or anything else that most people would rely on as the basis of a relationship. Penny Nichol Sherbino had gone to school with Art's younger sister, Jeannie, and she reminded him of Jeannie. Shawcross told the court-appointed psychiatrist for the prosecution that Penny was also a replacement—a sexual replacement for Jeannie—and that was the basis of the relationship. But the twice-divorced Shawcross seemed needy, and Penny Sherbino seemed more than capable of responding to his needs. Shawcross has called it a "convenient marriage." Five months into the marriage, Penny had a miscarriage, even though Shawcross said he rarely had sex with her and couldn't have an orgasm.

Shawcross met Penny Sherbino through his sister Jeannie, with whom, he told his psychiatrist, he was still having sexual relations even after he was released from Auburn. He said that Jeannie introduced him to Penny because Jeannie was pregnant by her boyfriend and couldn't fool around with Arthur any more.

"I was at my sister's apartment, fooling around with her," Shawcross said. "And that is when she told me she was pregnant and we couldn't do this no more. And I asked her if she knew anybody

233

where I could go to and she gave me Penny's name and her address. I called her up and Penny remembered me from high school and I went over. We just took off from there."

Shawcross said that he never actually had sexual intercourse with his sister. He has said that they fooled around by "fondling" one another or by having oral sex. Jeannie, Art has said, did not actually perform oral sex on him. Rather she allowed him to fondle her and perform oral sex on her. He also told psychiatrists that his sister was the only person who could excite him to climax by fondling his penis with her hand. Jeannie herself has consistently denied having any sexual relations with her brother. But, Shawcross said, after Jeannie told him she was pregnant, she got him Penny to replace her.

"When I got there to see Penny, it wasn't sexual. Nothing didn't come to mind and I went home. A couple of days later, I went back and we just started seeing each other on a regular basis. And she asked where I was and I told her I was in prison. We just hit it off. She had kids, a girl a year and a half and a boy three, maybe four. My marriage with her was okay except for one incident I had with her sister Rose—not my Rose. Penny was downtown with her mother and her sister was there with me and the two kids and I was upstairs in bed sleeping. She came upstairs and climbed in bed with me. And I told her no. And she was fifteen or sixteen years old and I thought more of her, and just explained it to her, 'No!' When Penny got home and her father walked in the door, the daughter, Jill, was sitting on the floor. He knew! I don't know how he knew, but he knew something went on. And he took me upstairs and talked to me and asked me and I told him. And then he takes Jill upstairs and talks to her. And he comes down and said, 'Thank you!' And went right out the door. But she and he came up every week to take care of the kids. My marriage to Penny broke up because I got arrested again."

Penny herself had dark memories of her marriage to Shawcross. She told the *Rochester Democrat and Chronicle* that she never loved Art and is happy that she miscarried his child and will never have to raise it. After the miscarriage, she remembers, Shawcross was arrested in the death of Karen Ann Hill and was implicated in the murder of Jack Blake. One of his closest friends, Penny remembers, Michael, with whom he used to fish with in nearby streams and ponds, years later killed his wife and children in Texas before shooting himself.

Shawcross's first civilian murder took place on June 4, 1972, while he was on his way to his stepson's birthday party. He had already been confronted by Penny's father about her teenaged sister climbing into his bed. He was already frustrated sexually because Penny was only a substitute for his sister Jeannie. But Shawcross hadn't had any more real sex since he had met Penny. Consequently, he was frustrated and angry on this June day as he trudged through the woods to the party.

"There was this one kid, he, he'd curse day in and day out. On this one day, I was ready to go to the party by a shortcut across a bunch of vacant lots instead of going through town, where my mother lived. Save four or five miles that way, 'cause you don't walk in the road. So I get set to leave and this kid comes to the door. Knocks on the door and asks if I want to go fishing. I said, 'No, I got to get to my wife's family.' And I closed the front door, and went out the back door, and I'm going across the back field to the shopping center.

"Now I'm going across the creek area, the swamp, and I get across the swamp and I hear a splash behind me. I turn around and there's that kid. He's following me. You know, how he got all the way around the housing project before I got out of sight, I don't know. And I went back and helped him out of the water. I told him, I says, 'Look, you can't go with me.' He starts cursing, he goes where he wants to. Nobody's going to stop him. So I just left him and climbed the cliff side on the other side of the swamp area there and crossed the tracks. I climbed over a . . . a barbed wire fence, and there's another swamp I had to go through. And I'm going through there, and then I hear a splash again, and he fell in the other swamp

236

across from the fence. And I'm getting *real* mad. I start swearing at him. I told him, 'You got to go home.' And says, 'I go where I want to.' And I just lost control. I hit him. I hit him right in the head with my fist. He fell down, and I left. And that afternoon I made it to my mother-in-law's for the birthday party and stuff."

As Shawcross had done so many times, he simply put the incident out of his mind. He told his doctors over and over again that when he doesn't like something, he just puts it out of his mind, he forgets about it, he lays it aside so it won't bother him. As intrigued and as fascinated as his doctors have been with his ability to forget things selectively, no one could deny that Shawcross was well-practiced at the art of denial. Denial was his way of getting through any difficult circumstances that had to be overcome. It is his way of staying in the flow of life without confronting the pain directly. Accordingly, Shawcross went to the party after assaulting Jack Blake and in his own mind denied that anything had ever happened.

"We got home about eleven o'clock. Later, it was probably about two or three in the morning, we get a knock at the door and the mother comes to the door wanting to know where her son was. I says, 'I ain't seen him since this morning.' And I knew inside, I knew he had to be still over there. So about three or four days went by and I just got up the nerve to go back and find out, but I didn't go the way I went the first time. I went, I came back from work, and I followed the railroad track out of town to that area, and he's still there in the water, and he was dead. I tried to cover him with leaves, then I left the area, went back to Watertown the same way I came in there. I was scared, but I just passed it out of my mind."

Shawcross explained that ever since he was ten and had been, in his own words, given oral sex by his aunt, he was able to deny reality, what was painful to him. "I just put it aside in my mind and forgot about it . . . anything that happened to me when I was a kid I just pushed things away."

Shawcross said that he went back to the Jack Blake remains a number of times to check on the condition of the body. "I went back there one time and there was nothing but bones," he told his psychiatrist. "There were no clothes on the skeleton, either. The second time I went back, I was talking to him. I told him how sorry I was, how I didn't mean it. I just couldn't face telling anybody about it." It was the first time he had told anyone that he had repeatedly visited the Blake remains.

The police had suspected that Shawcross had been back to the burial site because Jack's corpse was naked. The county medical examiner, Dr. Richard Lee, had suggested that the child had been forced to undress prior to the homicide and had been forced to run for a distance before he was killed or he had been undressed after he was killed.

The police also suspected that Blake was sexually molested.

Mary Blake, Jack Blake's mother, told the *Rochester Democrat and Chronicle* that she remembered Arthur Shawcross as the man who knocked on her front door four months before her son went over to play at the Cloverdale Apartments and never came back. She had seen Shawcross around town, "a man," the newspaper said, "who always rode a white bicycle with a white basket." Mary remembered that Shawcross showed up at the Blake residence to ask Jack and his brother Peter to go fishing. She told the boys that she didn't want them to go. She remembers warning Jack and Peter that "he could take you and I wouldn't know where you are going," she was quoted as saying. "Mom, he's my friend, he wouldn't hurt us," Jack was quoted in the paper as having told his mother. Shawcross, Mary remembers, stood in the doorway watching the exchange. He didn't say a word at first. Then he told Jack that he had to respect his mother's wishes.

Mary also remembered that a week before Shawcross showed up at her door, he had seen Jack and Peter playing ball and had asked them to go fishing with him on the Black River. They went along but came back from the river with a frightening story of what Shawcross had told them about Vietnam and what he threatened to do to Peter. Jack said that Shawcross told him and his brother

239

that he was hit by shrapnel in Vietnam and suffered from blackouts because of his wound. He also showed them pictures of naked women on the way home from the fishing spot. Jack got scared, he told his mother, and ran down the railroad tracks. Art, however, picked up his brother Peter by his pants and dangled him over an incline—he was going to drop him, Jack told his mother, unless Jack came back. The three of them went back to Watertown without having caught any fish. People last saw Jack Blake talking to Shawcross at the Cloverdale Apartments on the day Jack disappeared.

Shawcross became Mary's prime suspect in Blake's disappearance, she said, after she realized that Jack was missing. But when she reported her suspicions to the police, they dismissed them and suspected her instead. She said that the cops searched her basement for the remains of Jack's body for a week. Paul Browne, a reporter for the Watertown daily *Times,* who covered the investigation of the Blake and Hill murders, said that at the time, Mary Blake was under suspicion for the disappearance of her child because her family had previously had problems with law enforcement authorities. This also came to light in a series of interviews conducted by the *Rochester Democrat and Chronicle* into Shawcross's background after his arrest in Monroe County. Blake's body was discovered four months later, after Shawcross led police investigators to the spot.

Shawcross told his medical investigators in Rochester years later that the death of Jack Blake was an accident. He never meant to kill him, only to get him to go home. But he lost control, he said, just as he had lost control countless times when the urge to strike back at things that weren't going his way came over him. Even at Green Haven years later, his prison psychoanalysts would write that Shawcross had "poor impulse control." He would admit to Dr. Park Deitz and to the police that it was his inability to control his feelings that resulted in the sudden inclination to choke the prostitutes who challenged him and the other women who threatened him with disclosure.

Back in Watertown, in the early seventies, people remembered Shawcross as a guy who acted strange. The *Rochester Democrat and Chronicle* reported that Watertown residents remember Shawcross as a guy who liked to paint and fish and actually liked to be around children. But he also had a "reputation," his neighbors reported, especially during the times he was jailed for burglary and arson.

The Jefferson County sheriff, Don Newberry, was quoted by the papers as saying that Shawcross was "real creepy to children." He said, "He was known to stuff grass and leaves down [children's] pants," referring to an incident in Watertown shortly before the murder of Karen Ann Hill in which Shawcross stuffed lawn clippings down the pants of one of the neighborhood kids. "This was a daily thing," Newberry said, "roll around on the ground with them, wrestle with them, hang onto them."

One of Shawcross's neighbors who lived across the street from Arthur and Penny in the low-income Cloverdale Apartment projects said she remembered that Art would "sit in the middle of the housing project lawn—he was out there with his chair and little easel. . . . he'd sit outside and paint. The kids would flock around him, wondering what he was doing." She said this in an interview with the *Democrat and Chronicle* after Shawcross was arrested in Rochester for the prostitute murders.

The neighbor, Carol Lutz, said she saw Shawcross stuff grass down the six-year-old boy's pants and also into his mouth. It was a grim foreshadowing, local police would eventually learn of the living burial of Karen Ann Hill, who Shawcross suffocated by stuffing wet leaves and grass into her mouth. Even the parole officers who supervised Shawcross's release sixteen years later were horrified at the death of Karen Ann Hill.

"What the hell's he doing?" she remembers asking herself as she watched him wrestle the little boy, Michael Norfolk, to the ground, put grass clippings down his pants, and stuff them into his mouth. Penny Sherbino remembers that Shawcross spanked the little child as well. The Norfolk boy

242

complained to his mother, who reported the incident to the police. Shawcross confessed to police about what he did, but the parole board dismissed the incident as trivial, even though they wrote a misconduct report on him. He was fined ten dollars in Watertown city court and released.

Carol Lutz also told the newspaper that she remembered an incident in which he picked up her own six-year-old by his neck. There was something unsettling about his demeanor, she said in an interview. Though he seemed soft-spoken and mild, there was just something about him, "even just his looks," she was quoted by the newspaper as saying, "his eyes, you could just tell he was strange. Those eyes. There was something about his eyes—weird."

Three months after he murdered Blake, and while the police were still searching for the little boy's body, Shawcross came upon Karen Ann Hill while he was fishing at the Black River. He told police at first that he was mad at her for going down to the river alone. It was dangerous. He told Dr. Park Dietz, however, that something came over him. "I was just thinking about Jeannie," he said, reminding Dietz about his sister, "and this girl showed up. And it was just at that moment when I didn't hear nothing around me. And it was like the daylight got brighter and I just grabbed this little girl. All I could see was my sister Jeannie. I strangled her. I raped her, and I left."

Shawcross also told other investigators that after

243

he had raped Karen Ann Hill, she started crying and bleeding. Shawcross told the police that he was afraid, afraid of the crying and afraid of the disclosure. He strangled her, he told the cops. He strangled her after he had sex with her and then while she was still breathing, he suffocated her by stuffing leaves, river grass, and mud in her nose and mouth. He had pulled her shirt over her head and covered her body with large flat stones. He buried her—left her is a more accurate description—under a section of the Pearl Street Bridge over the Black River. Only her hair, hands, and feet were exposed. People had seen Shawcross and the Hill child together and had seen Shawcross's white bike by the Black River near the Pearl Street Bridge. Shawcross had also been seen by the bridge.

Sergeant John Dawley recalled to the *Democrat and Chronicle* that he was having dinner on September 3, 1972, when he got a call from Detective Charlie Kubinsky, who told him that the parolee Arthur Shawcross was a suspect in the Karen Ann Hill murder. He told the sergeant that a neighborhood girl saw Shawcross's white bike and Shawcross, eating ice cream, right over the bridge on the very day the body was discovered. The two police officers interrogated Shawcross for the better part of a day, confronting him with the facts in the case and laying out their suspicions for him. Finally, the detectives were quoted as saying

244

Shawcross said to them, "What's going to happen to me if I tell you something?"

With the detectives' ears perked up and with Shawcross's public defense lawyer firmly in control, Shawcross negotiated a plea-bargain with the Jefferson County district attorney's office in return for pleading guilty to one count of manslaughter in the death of Karen Ann Hill. Prosecutors, the District Attorney claimed afterward, had no direct evidence to connect Shawcross to the Blake murder and had no witnesses to the Hill rape. Therefore they were unable to charge Shawcross directly with rape or with a double count of homicide even though the parole board, they believed, would be able to consider the sexual offense and double homicide charges when Shawcross came up for parole.

At the time, Watertown residents remembered, the city was so shaken by the Blake murder that when Shawcross eventually confessed to the crime four months later, after he was in jail in the Karen Ann Hill murder, people believed that if Shawcross had been apprehended for the Blake murder, Karen Ann Hill would still be alive. "This case just overwhelmed the town," reporter Paul Browne told the *Rochester Democrat and Chronicle*. Some people urged that the state investigate the way the police handled the case because of the lack of aggressiveness on the part of the department after Blake disappeared. People said that Mary Blake had made her suspicions known to the police and had identi-

245

fied Shawcross as one of the few adults who had had any dealings with her son. She told them about the dirty pictures, she said, and she said that he had actually threatened Peter in order to control Jack. The police were also aware that Shawcross was a parolee who had already been cited for misconduct when he had manhandled the Norfolk child. There were simply too many circumstantial factors to implicate Shawcross in the Blake disappearance for the police not to have acted.

Surprisingly, it was only after Karen Ann Hill disappeared and the same people began focusing their attention on Shawcross that the prosecutors came up with the deal to plea-bargain away the Blake murder in exchange for Shawcross's confession. Perhaps it was the viciousness of the Karen Ann Hill murder or the way Shawcross disposed of the body that aroused the ire of so many people . . .

"Thing was, I couldn't hear no sounds when I saw the girl," Shawcross said to Dr. Dietz, "and the daylight got brighter and all I could see was my sister Jeannie. That happened when she came underneath the bridge. I just remember myself back when I was the same age."

Shawcross said that it was the oral sex he claimed to have had with his sister that filled his mind when he began fondling Karen Ann Hill. "I had oral sex with her, then I raped her, then, seein' what I did, I strangled her. She was scared. She was screaming. She looked like my sister, and I couldn't do nothing because of the brightness. Then the brightness started to leave me and I was seein' what I had done and I just backed off and caved in the bank on top of her. I pulled the rocks down, the sod loose from the side of the riverbank, and put it on top of her. Then I left."

Shawcross said that he fled the site almost immediately. He went through the back streets of Watertown, streets that he had come to know well, and wound his way back home. Shawcross said that he modified the appearance of his bicycle so that people wouldn't recognize it and that he was scared when the police came around asking him about the disappearance of the Hill girl and the Blake boy. "I was scared," he said, "because I knew where he was. Or I thought I knew where he was at that time."

Finally Shawcross told the prosecution psychiatrist in Monroe County that he was convinced that he would not have killed Jack Blake and Karen Hill had it not been for Vietnam. "Vietnam taught me how to kill," he said. It was the first place where he achieved a degree of sexual thrill out of having intercourse with his victims prior and subsequent to murdering them and butchering their remains. In a letter he wrote as a supplement to his journal for his medical investigators, he said that he did, in fact, have sex with the remains of Jack Blake and with the remains of most of the murdered women in Rochester. But he went much further and confirmed many of the police suspicions that he perpetrated far more mutilation on the bodies of all his victims than he previously admitted to.

"When Jack Blake followed me across a swamp and over the railroad tracks plus into some woods, I couldn't take it any longer. Telling him to go back. I did hit him in the throat and head, then strangled him. I had the same effect as here in Rochester because I cut parts of him out and ate them. I took his penis, balls, and heart and ate them. Why I did this I don't know. I also had sex with his body. I had sex with all the girls' bodies and even slept next to them for a while. I'll not talk or explain any of this to anyone. I don't know why, but I cannot."

In 1972, Arthur Shawcross was convicted of one count of manslaughter in the death of Karen Ann Hill and sentenced to prison for twenty-five years. He was not charged with rape and he was not tried for the murder of Jack Blake. The parents of the victims were told not to worry about Shawcross's getting out of jail and killing anyone else. The parole board, they were told, would see to it that a man like Shawcross who had committed such heinous crimes and who had committed them while he was already on probation for arson would have to serve his full term. It would be a different Arthur Shawcross who would return from prison, the parents were told. No one would ever have anything to fear from Shawcross again when the gates of Green Haven closed behind him for the last time.

At least that's what everyone thought.

Chapter 14
Hard Time

"The first eight years were hard for me," Shawcross told investigators after he was arrested for the Rochester prostitute murders. He went to the New York State Penitentiary at Green Haven after pleading guilty to a single count of manslaughter. The other prisoners had heard about his reputation as a child killer and gave him a very hard time about it. There is very little respect for child killers or child molesters behind prison walls—the inmates call them "short eyes"—and child killers often have to fight simply to stay alive.

Shawcross said that he had gotten into fights at Green Haven because he had to protect himself. Inmates picked fights with him in the yard and threatened him whenever they could. When he was threatened directly, he said, he stood his ground and fought. When he felt inmates conspiring to kill him, he would refuse to leave his cell because it was the one place where he felt safe. In prison, he explained, other inmates will take whatever you don't defend. If you don't defend yourself, they will take you.

Shawcross said that he was prepared to defend himself. He also refused to be a loner in prison because they have especially difficult times. There was one incident, he described, in which three inmates beat him up at Green Haven. He attacked each of them individually and they threatened to have him killed. They were quickly transferred to Attica. He said that one of his inmate friends told him afterward that he had put the word out at Attica that there was a "contract" on these new transferees. Shortly thereafter, Shawcross said, state police investigators interrogated him about the deaths of these inmates and Shawcross's involvement in it.

"I told the investigators that I was here all the time and didn't know nothing about anybody dyin' in Attica. I spent my time there and wasn't there now."

That was the end of that incident. But there were other times, Shawcross said, when he refused to leave his cell because he knew there were death threats against him. At those times, guards would have to come in and remove him forcibly. Consequently, he was disciplined repeatedly during the first eight years for refusing to follow the guards' instructions.

The parole records assembled in his file provide a complete record of Shawcross's problems within the prison. Just two months into his sentence, a

1977 report notes, Shawcross was reported for talking after 7:30 P.M. when a silence period had been imposed. In May 1973, Shawcross was confined to jail for seven days after fighting with inmate #17935 after he claimed that he had entered the inmate's cell to repair a set of earphones when the inmate attacked him. In August 1973, Shawcross was "keeplocked" because he learned several inmates were out to "pipe" him and refused to leave his cell. When prison authorities appeared in order to escort him to a parole hearing, Shawcross refused to leave his cell and then set fire to his mattress. Shawcross said that inmates wanted to beat him with a pipe after news of his child murders appeared in a criminal magazine that had been circulating through the prison population. In September 1973, Shawcross was reported for running in the prison corridor; he refused to appear for a psychiatric interview in 1974, and on February 27, 1974, he was cited for having contraband items in his cell. Four months later he was cited again for stealing state food and three months after that he was cited for fighting with another inmate. He was sentenced to a thirty-day loss of all prison privileges. The following year he was attacked by another inmate and was released after a reprimand. Finally, in 1976, he was cited for having contraband food in his cell. He lost all privileges for twenty days.

By 1976, Shawcross said, his troubles began to

ease. He straightened out in prison, became more cooperative, and fought less with the other inmates and with prison authorities. As he settled in for the long haul, he sought work in prison, sought education, and generally made better appearances before the parole boards evaluating him every six months. His next seven years therefore went more smoothly, and he even became a model prisoner.

Shawcross said that he received little specialized therapy in prison. He was interviewed by prison psychologists repeatedly, but spent very little time in formal therapy sessions, he said. He was asked to participate in "group" over and over again, but he said that most of the people in group therapy were either "really crazy; like they weren't really there" or they were "mental retards." Being in therapy and trying to relate with people like this, Shawcross explained to prosescution psychiatrists, was deranging for him because he knew he wasn't "crazy like they were," but he knew he had problems.

He tried to explain to his prison therapists that Vietnam was a factor in his early crimes, but the therapists, he said, weren't prepared to talk about the war. Understandably, during the first few years of Shawcross's prison term, the United States was still fighting the war while trying to pull the troops out. The stories of post-traumatic stress among veterans and of the atrocities and violence that the troops had seen were still a few years away. Consequently, most of Shawcross's stories, whether real or fantasy, never seemed to make an impression on the mental health professionals he spoke to in prison.

For example, in one of his first psychological evaluations done in June 1973—only months after he arrived at Green Haven—Shawcross was not considered a psychological risk. "At present there is no evidence of hallucinations, delusions, sensory deceptions, and none could be elicited," Dr. Albert Dresser wrote. Even though the psychiatrist confirmed that Shawcross had reported "hearing voices" in the past, he was unable to be specific about what they said or what he heard. "He states that he has had auditory hallucinations only when he is depressed," the report continues. It states that the reason Shawcross is being interviewed and evaluated is because he himself requested it. "He wants to know why he committed the last crime and asked to see a psychiatrist." Dr. Dresser's report found no clinical evidence of mental illness in Shawcross but requested that medical examinations be scheduled and asked to see him again in the future.

Five months later, in October 1973, Shawcross was evaluated by prison psychologist J. R. McWilliams at the request of the prison administration. Dr. McWilliams administered a battery of standard psychological and cognitive tests including the Wechsler Adult Intelligence and the Bender Motor

Gestalt test. Dr. McWilliams said that he found no signs of neurological impairment and that Shawcross's memory appeared to be intact.

He further accurately reported that Shawcross "relied heavily upon fantasy as a source of satisfaction." McWilliams also reported that Shawcross revealed that he suffered from anxiety attacks. He tested out to a combined I.Q. of 99 which, McWilliams' reported, was in the normal adult range.

In the final section of his report, McWilliams suggests that Shawcross "seems to be a normal individual who knows he has done wrong and would like to help himself get back on the right track for his eventual return to society." However, after the underlined "normal individual," an unknown writer who had access to the McWilliams report penciled in the words "a psychopathic killer" in handwriting different from the psychologist's signature. This phrase would eventually come back to haunt the parole board years later when a parole officer in upstate New York remarked about them in his warning to other parole officers in the region prior to Shawcross's release from Green Haven. Whoever wrote that Shawcross was a psychopathic killer back in 1973 was truly prophetic. It is unfortunate that that diagnosis wasn't acted upon at that time.

In 1976, Michael Boccia wrote a slightly more critical psychological evaluation of Arthur Shawcross in which he described an inmate who had still not fully grasped the implications of the

crimes he had been punished for. Boccia said that
Shawcross still tended to blame others for his problems or blame the circumstances that surrounded
him. He said that the inmate had led an "aimless
existence" and had not yet come to terms with his
pedophilia and aberrant sexual behavior. Boccia
also disputes Shawcross's claim that he needed psychological intervention. He writes that in his opin-
ion, the only reason Shawcross requested the
psychological interview was to impress the parole
board, not to seek help. Shawcross himself has said
repeatedly that he sought help for his anxiety while
in Green Haven but was consistently denied therapy, especially therapy designed to remedy his sexual problems and his fantasies about violence. The
apparent misunderstanding between Shawcross and
Boccia here, as evidenced in Boccia's report, is sur-
prising in light of Shawcross's history prior to this
interview and what happened after he was paroled.

By 1977, Shawcross said that he had begun to
make an adjustment to prison life. He said that he
began pursuing his General Equivalency Diploma
to qualify him for employment after he left prison
and he was studying to be a locksmith. By 1975,
Shawcross said, he became the only licensed and
qualified locksmith in the entire prison—"the only
one the prison ever had." He said that for the first
time in his life, "I was doing something right for a
change for the next two years. I was sending to
Penn State University for lessons in horticulture.

Did a B average. Then I took a job working with mental patients, inmate counselor."

His psychological interview in June 1977 reflects his change of attitude. Dr. Y. A. Haveliwala, prison psychiatrist, reported that Shawcross had become more self-reflective over the two previous years and had adapted to the working conditions of prison. However, the psychiatrist wrote that Shawcross still reported having "terrifying nightmares" even though he did not have hallucinations. But, Haveliwala concluded, Shawcross had not resolved his psychosexual conflicts, he had low self-esteem, and his insight was "minimal." Haveliwala suggested that Shawcross had a schizoid personality, that he was antisocial, and that he had a definitive personality disorder. These in themselves are usually enough to red-flag an individual who has committed violent crimes and sexual crimes and who has set fires. In the case of Shawcross, a convicted child killer, they should have been enough to have mandated against his parole for more than the ten years he remained in prison after that report. Further, Haveliwala wrote, "This man does not show a good degree of evidence of successfully resolving or working out his psychosexual conflicts." These are menacing characteristics because they accurately predict that, confronted with a challenging problem that he can't work out, Shawcross will resort to the primal responses he learned so well in Vietnam and perpetrated so violently in Watertown.

257

Two years later, in a psychological parole report, Dr. Boyar wrote that although he was aware Shawcross was attempting to make a good showing for the purposes of impressing the parole board, the prisoner's speech nevertheless "did not indicate any homicidal or suicidal ideas at the present time." However, Boyar wrote, "it seems to this examiner that we are dealing with a person of abnormal character traits with psychosexual difficulties. It must be noted that the above-mentioned complications tend to be chronic in duration." Again, chronic psychosexual difficulties are not to be dismissed lightly. They tend to indicate that under the appropriate conditions, Shawcross could revert to the reactions that had landed him in jail in the first place. And that's exactly what happened ten years after the report was written.

In a parole hearing report written about the time of Boyar's evaluation, the caseworker seemed struck by a dual nature he observed in Shawcross's personality. He says that Shawcross had a very poor sense of his own masculinity because of the situation in his household after his mother's "abusive control over the inmate's father." Further, the writer states, "the inmate seems to have approached adolescence with no idea whatsoever of what sort of person he was or of the normal limits to be placed upon one's inner instincts." Worse, the parole board writer suggests, "Because of this inmate's early sexual stimulation and his weak personality structure, which is essentially unable to control his inner drives, for this inmate, sexual stimulation is as uncontrollable as heroin addiction might be in another; but because this inmate was brought up essentially by himself, his stimulations are likely to take a ruminative turn toward primal satisfaction and are likely to surface in a manner which will be found socially abhorrent." This sounds like a clear prediction of Shawcross's later crimes. But the writer is even more prophetic when he says that he does not feel that "the inmate has any conscious desire, when his blood is cool, to be a bad person or to hurt others. The inmate, however, has proved himself to be an extremely unusual person and one whose actual inner workings are probably completely beyond comprehension of any of us."

What the caseworker was suggesting, and what we later found to be the case, was that there were in fact two very different types of people living inside Arthur Shawcross, even though he was not a multiple personality. We would find in 1990 that Shawcross was typically a mild-mannered individual when not placed under any stress. But when stressed, physiological changes would take place very dramatically within his system which would rob him of any resiliency whatsoever and turn him into a slave to his primal sexual and violent impulses. This condition, which we would later see diagnosed as kryptopyroluria, was at the heart of Shawcross's post-traumatic stress condition. In

1979, however, all the caseworker could do was simply point to Shawcross's behavior. Again, it is unfortunate that this observation was buried under piles of subsequent paperwork because it actually predicts the kinds of crimes that Shawcross was capable of perpetrating when under stress.

By 1981, a very different Shawcross was evaluated for a subsequent parole hearing by psychiatrist Ismail Ozyaman. In this interview, Dr. Ozyaman describes an inmate with good self-esteem and a good self-image who expresses remorse and regret over his crimes and evidences a clear contact with reality. He is described as demonstrating that he is well-oriented, capable of progressing logically from one point to the next, and absent any hallucinatory experiences. He has no delusions about himself, Dr. Ozyaman writes, and is able to give a rational account of his past. Gone from this report are stories about haunting nightmares and powerful psychosexual feelings that the inmate is unable to resolve. Here is an inmate well able to leave prison, according to the implications of the report, as long as he is placed within some kind of mental care facility that will monitor him. "He is in good control of his mental faculties," Dr. Ozyaman states. He does not address previous reports of Shawcross's antisocial personality and personality disorder other than to note them in his introduction. Also, fascinatingly enough, Dr. Ozyaman writes that Shawcross told him that he tried to enter the military service but "could not pass the entrance examination."

Throughout this period, Shawcross was repeatedly denied his applications for parole at hearing after hearing. He first became eligible for parole five years into his 25-year sentence after his first appearance before a parole board on September 20, 1973. Subsequently, according to parole board records, Shawcross was placed into the Accelerated Release Procedure Program and was given a conditional release date of May 2, 1989.

He was first reviewed for parole in June, 1977, after he had spent the requisite five years of his prison sentence. At that time, the parole board read into the record a letter from the Jefferson County District Attorney which described the seriousness of Shawcross's crimes, noted that he had committed these crimes while on parole from burglary and arson charges, and pleaded with the parole board not to release Shawcross until the full term of his sentence was carried out. District Attorney Lee Clary wrote, "I cannot express strongly enough my feelings and the feelings of the people of Jefferson County in opposing a release of Arthur Shawcross . . . if this man is released, no one in this county will have any faith in the criminal justice system."

The parole board took Lee Clary at his word and held Shawcross over for subsequent hearings. However, the parole board noted that Shawcross was honorably discharged from the Army with a rank of Spec. 4. This makes Dr. Ozyaman's reference to Shawcross's inability to pass the Army entrance examinations all the more distressing because Shawcross's previous parole hearing records should have been available to the psychiatrist who was reporting on the inmate's qualifications for parole ten years later.

Dr. Ozyaman also interviewed Shawcross two years later for a subsequent parole hearing and found him to be still in good contact with reality and suffering from no emotional instability. "He is in good control of his mental faculties," Dr. Ozyaman writes, "and does not manifest any psychotic or neurotic symptomatology." Although the psychiatrist gives him a generally clean bill of emotional health, he suggests that Shawcross's problems might be chronic and that they might recur under the appropriate circumstances. "There is always the possibility of recurrence of poor impulse control, and acting under past emotional conflicts under the stress of this type of case."

Two years later, however, in preparation for his 1985 parole board hearing, Shawcross was given a very positive psychological evaluation. Dr. Charles Chung, the evaluating psychiatrist, and Dr. Michael Boccia both stated that Shawcross "does not exhibit emotional disturbance."

The parole board, meeting the following month, also noted that Shawcross had followed the prerequisite course of self-improvement in order to qualify for parole. Shawcross himself told the board that "I have done what the commissioners asked me to do. Different types of programs I have done. My school education. I got my high school education. Clean record. I have started college courses from Penn State University. I have two therapy classes, one under Agent Orange and another one under the PSU here. I want to know if there is anything else you people want me to do."

"Part of what we do with you is based upon our conversations here," Commissioner Mulholland told Shawcross. "Do you want to talk about the past incidents that brought you here?"

"My past I can't dispute," Shawcross said. "Now I find out these things came out of my past as a child, plus things I did overseas. At that time, I couldn't talk about it. Numerous counselors and psychologists in here and even the officers I have talked to would bring everything out. I am responsible for what I did and I regret it. Nothing I can do about it."

"You've spent half your adult life in here," Mulholland said. "What was going in your head that time that would cause you to get into that kind of behavior?"

"I was having a lot of problems when I came back to this country from Vietnam," Shawcross told the board. "I couldn't work a full day. And I was just restless. Couldn't sleep that good. And

263

things were just piling up on me. And I don't know what led me."

"Do you think it was sort of a post-traumatic stress combat thing?" Mulholland asked.

"Well, sir, we did things in Vietnam that were pretty hideous, you know? It was partly that. It was partly things that happened in my home when I was a kid."

Commissioner Mulholland again brought up Shawcross's murder of the two children, whereupon Shawcross became silent.

Mulholland reminded Shawcross that when psychiatrists previously asked Shawcross about the murder of the children, he was unable to respond. This time, Mulholland asked, what could Shawcross say about them? Why had he not been able to talk about his crimes to psychologists previously?

"I don't remember," Shawcross told him. "I don't recall."

"Did the youngster die by your hand?" Mulholland asked again.

"Yes sir," Shawcross replied, but he had nothing else to say.

The parole board denied his early release and remanded him to a hearing before the 1987 board, when he would normally be released under the Accelerated Release Program. However, the board went further. In a decision dated July 18, 1985, they wrote, "Furthermore, his belligerent reaction

264

represents a foreboding potential for a possible re-enactment of his tragic behavior. This writer additionally questioned the inmate regarding his lack of participation in Special Treatment Programming during the last two years and especially the absence of Sex Offender Programming. The inmate responded to the effect that 'Group therapy does not work.' A continuation of the topic germinated and the inmate in a fury left the interview. As a result, the interview was not completed. Though the psychiatric and psychological profession has apparently not as of yet defined a diagnosis for this inmate's aberrant behavior or even more pertinently a cure, the society at large deserves protection until such is the case, which probably would not be until well past this inmate's conditional release date. Consequently this writer recommends a 24-month hold with recommendation for the Sex Offender and other psychotherapeutic programming which this inmate has recently deemed unbeneficial."

Arthur Shawcross was granted a parole from Green Haven in March 1987, and was released into the Binghamton community.

Chapter 15
On Parole

"At the risk of being dramatic," Robert T. Kent, Senior Parole Officer for the Binghamton Sub Area Office, wrote in a memo to Area Supervisor De-Gennaro in Elmira on May 6, 1987, about parolee Arthur Shawcross, "the writer considers this man to be possibly the most dangerous individual to have been released to this community in many years. As a result I feel compelled to make him the subject of this special memorandum to you, especially since there are no longer dual folders kept in the Elmira office and you would not otherwise be aware of this individual."

Kent explains that part of the reason for Shawcross's potential danger is the nature of the arrangement he made with the prosecution which allowed him to receive a relatively light sentence for the crimes he actually committed. Kent suggests that under more "typical" circumstances, someone who had committed the murders that Shawcross confessed to would have received a far stiffer sentence and would be in jail until he was much older. Shawcross, he says, served only fifteen years on a manslaughter "one" when in actuality he was a multiple-homicide offender as well as a child killer and molester. "He is currently serving a 25-0-0 year term for manslaughter in the first degree, having been sentenced out of Jefferson County after what appears to be an incredible plea bargaining arrangement. Shawcross admits the murder of two young children in two separate incidents."

Kent explains that the case aroused great anguish in Jefferson County, not only because of the nature of the crime, but because some of the details of the crime never came out. "Although the case folder is quite thick, many key details seem to be missing concerning the crime. However, it is known that on 9/2/72, in the City of Watertown, New York, the body of an eight-year-old girl was found lying facedown in the dirt under a bridge. Only her hair and her hands and feet were exposed, since large flat stones had been piled on top of the body. The case folder makes references to the fact that the girl was sexually molested and/or raped and her mouth was wide open and packed with dirt from the area. Her nostrils were also packed with dirt, and it appears that she suffocated as a result of this."

Bob Kent explains that Shawcross confessed to this murder after the police investigation identified him as a suspect. One of the items in that investigation, Shawcross's parole violation report for 1972 states, was that the local Watertown Police investigator, Detective Charles Kubinski, had used bloodhounds to retrace what he assumed to be the murderer's steps from the scene of Karen Ann Hill's burial directly to the Cloverdale Apartment unit where Shawcross lived. Shawcross told Kubinsky that he couldn't remember any of the details in the girl's murder, but that he must have done it. Shawcross said that he had completely blacked out the time that he had spent with the girl. This information was in Shawcross's parole file, in his "report of violation of parole," over the signatures of Edward L. Yanchitis, Area Supervisor, and Lyle W. Sylver, Parole Officer, and it was dated November 1, 1972.

"On 9/6/72," Kent's memo continues, "the skeletal remains of a ten-year-old boy were found and Shawcross subsequently admitted to murdering the boy by bludgeoning him on the head. The only information available was Shawcross's statement, and he indicated that the boy was following him and when he refused to stop following him he struck him on the head, causing his death. He also covered the body of this boy with bark and debris from the area. This murder was committed four months prior to the murder of the young girl and occurred some time around 5/7/72."

When I reviewed these portions of Kent's memos prior to my own investigation, I was particularly taken aback by the similar profiles of Shawcross's crimes in Watertown, his descriptions of what he claimed to have done in Vietnam (remember, I was treating these as fantasies and not as true events), and his murders of the eleven prostitutes in Rochester. In every incident, with the exception of the murder of Jack Blake, Shawcross murdered his female victims in the act of or immediately after raping them. In every incident he later claimed to have had sex with or to have slept beside the remains. Subsequently Shawcross claimed to have had sex with Jack Blake's remains and to have covered Jack's body with debris and bark, just as he had covered Karen Ann Hill and some of his Rochester victims. He also claimed to have devoured parts of his victims from all three separate murder sprees. In other words, the crime scene profiles match in all three instances, even if the victim profiles do not indicate a *prima facie* match. In reality, all the victim profiles really do match, but I wouldn't discover that until many months later.

Kent was particularly struck by the fact that Shawcross committed the two murders while he was already on parole for burglary and arson. To a parole officer, it stands to reason that once a parolee violates his probation, his credibility with respect to adhering to parole rules is tainted. So it was with Shawcross, Kent indicates in his memo.

"Of particular importance is the fact that Shawcross was serving a prison term for Burglary

269

in the 3rd Degree at the time and was on parole supervision. His criminal history dates back to 1963, when he was arrested for Burglary in the 3rd Degree but was adjudicated a Youthful Offender and placed on Probation. He was arrested in 1965 for Burglary in the 2nd degree, but this was reduced to Unlawful Entry and he was sentenced to six months probation. In 1969 he was arrested for Burglary and Arson, 2nd degree, but he subsequently pled guilty to the previously mentioned burglary 3rd charge and received a 5-0-0 year State Prison term. Of concern is the fact that in the case folder there is a written statement that he gave following his arrest for Arson and in that statement he admits that he intentionally started a fire at a paper company [Knowltons Brothers] where he worked in Watertown. He also admitted to setting fire to a barn and causing $5,000 worth of damage there and subsequently set a fire at a milk plant [Crowley] where he went to work after he left the paper company."

Kent quite correctly makes the connection between Shawcross's previous sexual problems and his firesetting. He points to problems that Shawcross has had with children in the past as a potential indicator of what might have happened in Watertown in 1972. "The case folder indicates that he had some sexual problems with his second wife and that he was apparently sexually drawn to his fifteen-year-old sister-in-law. He also apparently ad-

270

mitted to an institutional Parole Officer that he had been sexually intimate with his sister during the ages of approximately twelve or thirteen."

In fact, Shawcross told Dr. Park Dietz three years after Kent wrote this memo that he began a sexual relationship with his sister when he was ten and she was seven by introducing her to fondling and oral sex. He maintained to Dr. Dietz that he continued fondling her sexually and that she allowed him to fondle her sexually continuously — before and after his tour of duty in the Army — up until she became pregnant and introduced him to his third wife, Penny. If what Shawcross told Dr. Dietz for the prosecution, Dr. Dorothy Ottnow Lewis for the Monroe County defense, Dr. Russell Barton also for the prosecution, and myself for the defense in Wayne County is true, then Shawcross — from the time he was a small child and unable to defend his boundaries — had integrated a sexual stimulation response into his way of dealing with emotional defenses. This was entirely unnatural and lies at the heart of many of Shawcross's problems. Therefore for Kent to have represented Shawcross's sexual problems as prominently as he did in his report was entirely correct and should have been a red flag for the entire parole team that managed Shawcross's case. Unfortunately, Kent's admonitions regarding Shawcross were not heeded.

Kent cited the 1979 Green Haven institutional Parole Summary that referenced Shawcross's aberrant sexual maturity, his arson, his sexual crimes, and his primal responses toward stress and cited that prediction that Shawcross might well turn out to display "socially abhorrent" behavior in response to negative stimulation. He also cited those evaluations which pointed to Shawcross's "poor impulse control" and his "schizoid personality" and pointed to the fact that psychiatrists had noted his "psychosexual difficulties." Kent was trying to make the Elmira office as aware as possible that although Shawcross had been paroled and had satisfied the requirements of his sentence under law, he was still potentially a danger to others if he was not managed properly.

Part of the problem, Kent wrote, was that he could not be returned to the Watertown area because of his own wishes and the wishes of the community. "The community at large was very much opposed to him returning there," Kent wrote. He suggested placing Shawcross in the Binghamton area because although Shawcross had continued a "pen-pal" relationship with Rose Walley over the years and had indicated that the two of them would live together and get married, Rose lived in Delaware County, an area that was too remote. Kent believed that Shawcross needed much closer supervision and management. Therefore, Kent suggested, the Binghamton area, with its medical and counseling facilities, was the better placement area for Arthur Shawcross.

272

The parole board developed what Kent called a "semistructured" plan for Shawcross, requiring him to participate in a mental health counseling program with a once-a-week report schedule, confine his movements to Broome County, observe an 11 P.M. to 7 A.M. curfew, refrain from drinking any alcoholic beverages, and refrain from having any contact with anyone under the age of eighteen. It ordered that he stay away from schools and schoolyards and not loiter in areas where children might be present, and that he discuss with his parole officer those specific conditions under which contact between himself and a child might arise. These rigorous conditions, the parole board felt, would prevent Shawcross from experiencing the kinds of stimulation which might interfere with his rehabilitation. However, the Shawcross release plan ran into difficulties almost immediately after his parole.

When Gerald Szachara notified the Binghamton Police Department of Shawcross's placement in the community, he was faced with negative questions from the officers. They asked, Kent wrote DeGennaro, why Shawcross was paroled in the first place if the parole board had such doubts about his abilities on the outside that they prohibited him from having contact with children. Sergeant David Lindsey of the Binghamton Police Department, the father of a young girl who was molested and murdered, confronted Shawcross when he was fishing by one of the local parks and "pointed out to him that he [Lindsey] just wanted to see what he looked like." Lindsey eventually visited the parole office to get more information about Shawcross. Sergeant Lindsey also requested — and his request was granted — that Shawcross be prohibited from going into the park that was named after Lindsey's murdered daughter. After Lindsey's visit, two Binghamton detectives visited Shawcross and told him they wanted to see what he looked like. "This has made Shawcross extremely nervous, but to his credit he has been most cooperative with us," Kent wrote.

Kent also pointed out that the parole department had a dual responsibility. Obviously they were required to protect the community from Shawcross, but at the same time they were required to protect Shawcross from the community. "We felt that it was imperative to make the Binghamton Police aware of Shawcross's presence here because of the high potential risk that he presents. However, we certainly do not want him to be harassed by the local police."

Bob Kent realized that Shawcross presented a danger to the community. He'd already seriously violated his parole once and there were no guarantees that he wouldn't violate it again. Kent simply had to walk the very fine line between letting the law work to *protect* Shawcross and protecting the community *from* Shawcross. It wasn't an easy job, and Kent's memo shows that he had his work laid out

274

for him. In his own way and within the administrative limits of his job, Kent presented the central problem that confronts all officers of the court. Kent tried heroically to balance what turned out to be conflicting points of view. It's a task that confronts most parole officers every day on the job. In the Shawcross case, it was unfortunate that the red flags of danger weren't recognized years before because Shawcross represents the type of individual most in need of serious and dramatic intervention.

In his own words, Arthur Shawcross was a cauldron of fury when he began his parole. As he explained it to Park Dietz, the appearances of the uniformed Binghamton Police officers forced him out of the town of Binghamton. He had made plans to stay with Rose Walley, his pen-pal and soon-to-be wife, up north in Delhi, New York, where she had an apartment. She had already cleared Shawcross's staying in her apartment with the landlady, Shawcross told Dietz, but when he got there, fireworks began almost immediately.

"She had an apartment up there and she told the landlady that she had somebody coming up to live with her. 'Okay. He doesn't have to sign the lease or nothing.' So when I got there the same morning, I went down to see the landlady and she said, 'You don't have to sign the lease. She already signed it. It's already talked over.' But during the week, the chief of the Delhi Police, he goes in and contacts the newspaper, contacts everybody in town. That's not something he's supposed to do. So things started getting hot down there. The landlady, she comes up and tells Rose that she's got to move because she didn't tell her that I was coming. But that was a lie."

Shawcross had now been chased out of two communities. He was nervous, he was on edge, he had resolved none of his problems with violence while in therapy in prison. He had, I believe, a serious problem coping with stress of any type. The man had absolutely no resiliency and no ability — *chemically* no ability — to withstand any stressful situation without exploding into violence. He was completely at sea. Now the parole board allowed him to live in the cellar of the First Baptist Church in Delhi. He was almost a refugee.

"We stayed in the First Baptist Church, in the cellar, a day or so. And then there was a Walton reporter with a camera kept chasing everybody. And if me and Rose went to go out of the church, he'd be running around the corner with a camera. Finally I had to call the state police. You couldn't call the cops in Delhi so you call the state police. So the state police chased the camera with this guy away. He was invading privacy. Now half the church was divided about us. I enjoyed going to church. Even when I was in prison I went to church, the Baptist church. I got out and I wanted to start things over. People wouldn't let me. That's another 'push.' They just wouldn't let me. The church preaches one thing, but the people in the church talk another.

"So I got chased out of the church and the minister found us a place in Fleischmanns, New York. Now that was a beautiful house, and I had a job. I was working with a contractor putting up siding and painting houses. And it was a two-story house and it was eleven bedrooms and two kitchens, two bathrooms, and it was furnished. It was over-furnished. It belonged to a man from New York and he says we could rent it year round if we wanted it. He'd only show up one or two months of the year.

"So by the time—the middle of the week—Rose and I walked down to the little village post office, I was going to sign for a post office box. The woman behind the screen, she recognized my picture from the *Walton Times* or something and says 'You're not getting no mail here.' So she contacts the mayor of the town. The sheriff drops by and tells Rose that there is a lynch mob coming to kick me out of town. The mayor was leading them. I refused to move. A bunch of people in front of the apartment threatened to burn me out. They threatened to hang me and all this stuff here. We were scared, sure. Then the people got out in front with flashlights and torches. They started screaming my name to come outside. I had all the lights out. I opened that front door and one guy started talking, making threats. I made one statement: who-

277

ever made one step into that yard was a dead man. Whoever: man, woman, or child. That stopped them for a while. And the Walton reporter showed up the next day all by himself. And he's across the road. He gets out of the car. He's got someone in the car with him. He comes across the road. He gets on the property, and I told him, I says, 'You come anywhere near this house and I'll blow you straight across that road.' He didn't know I had a gun. We didn't have one, but he went back down the road."

Shawcross said that he bluffed the reporter away, but the reporter related the threat to the state police, who showed up later that night. Had they found a gun, Shawcross would have been in violation of his parole. But he allowed them to search. He had been through another possibly life-threatening situation in a confrontation with the police and with an angry mob who had surrounded him and Rose. Shawcross felt fear not only for himself but also for Rose, whom he had induced to join him. Now she was in jeopardy because of him. And because of what Shawcross had said to the mob and to the reporter, he had placed himself at risk for violating his parole.

"The state police said, 'You threatened to kill this man.' I says, 'Yeah, he's threatening me, but there's no gun in the house. Go look.' They go look and everything. They can't find nothing. So that night the state police showed up back at the house. They say my parole officer says 'We got to take you to Binghamton.' I says, 'I'm not leaving.' I says, "I'm not leaving Rose here. Where I go, Rose goes.' I says, 'If she don't go, I'm not going.' So he left and came back with another state trooper and they took both of us and a few bags of stuff that we had and left."

Shawcross was extremely protective of Rose Walley at this point not only because she was loyal to him, but because he realized that she had already left her own husband to join him upon his release. Rose had nowhere else in the world to go, and Shawcross suddenly found himself in the position of managing Rose's life only days out of being released from a prison situation where his own life was completely managed. It was an extremely stressful situation, building to greater levels of stress with every confrontation. The presence of the police and of guns and of crowds and threatening local reporters looking for a "no-brainer" story was ultimately building to a head. It was the Baptist minister, the Reverend Lawrence Duthie, who turned out to be one of the very few heroes, along with Bob Kent, in the entire Shawcross saga. Reverend Duthie told the newspapers that Shawcross "was just trying to get along as best he could."

"The minister made arrangements with another minister. He came back there with his van. He took all our stuff and took it back to the church and put it in the cellar until we got relocated. Then they brought us to Binghamton. And a parole officer there stuck us in a hotel in Vestal, New York. They told us to stay there until further notice, then they came and they says 'We're going to take you to Utica.' Okay, so we start going up through New York and ended up in Elmira and we got the place in Elmira, the house up there."

But if Shawcross thought that his troubles were now over, he was mistaken. "Now they wanted to separate me from Rose. I says, 'I'm not going for it.' Then they said they are going to take me to Rochester. I didn't want to come here. I liked the country. I didn't like city life. So they convinced us to go here anyway. So when we got to Rochester, at the parole office here on Court Street, they took us to a group home, a mental group home on Clinton and Westcott Street. They put us in an apartment that was completely furnished. Nice apartment. Didn't lack for nothing. They bought the groceries. All you had to do was stay in there, stay out of sight. Great! That's just what we did."

What Shawcross didn't know was that the parole board had had enough. They realized that wherever they placed the man, he was going to run into trouble. Kent had accurately predicted that Shawcross presented a real conflict to the higher-ups in the parole system. If Shawcross had a right to be on the outside—and according to the law he had that right—then he had a right to be protected. If that right to be protected was in direct conflict

280

with the community's need to have parolees in their jurisdictions identified, then someone's right was going to have to be compromised. The Division of Parole decided to compromise the rights of the community.

In fact, three days before Shawcross arrived in Rochester, according to the *Rochester Democrat and Chronicle,* Executive Director of the New York State Division of Parole Edward Elwin urged that parole officials maintain confidentiality over the placement of parolees. Because he was afraid that the community interest in parole releases might jeopardize the rights of parolees, Elwin wrote the parole board chairman, Ramon J. Rodriguez on June 26, 1987 that it was imperative that New York State resist the requests of the community to know who was being placed in their jurisdictions.

But after protecting Shawcross in privacy at the mental health center, the parole board moved him to a new location. "The next morning the people who ran the house took us out of there, stuck us into a shell of an apartment, no stove, no refrigerator, nothing. Didn't even have a bed in there. They says, 'This is what we're going to give you.' Now the state's paying $550 a month for my rent. Rose and I had to go get a job somewhere in town to pay her rent. That's over a thousand dollars a month. And they stick us in an empty apartment. We stuck it out for two months. We got ourselves a job and we moved over on Alexander Street."

Shawcross had effectively moved out of his supervised situation, he claims, not because he wanted to go underground but because he couldn't afford to remain supervised in the apartment that was provided for him. Gradually, however, they were able to furnish their apartment by "curbing," removing articles left on the curb as garbage by other people. "We get furniture in the curb. We use a shopping cart, find a couch, nothing wrong with it. Bring it home. Then, when we made friends with people with a pickup truck, we went two loads. We were able to get a bigger apartment for the same rent we were paying for the studio, but it was bigger. Now we have a nice place to stay and we were a thousand dollars ahead in rent."

Shawcross got a job working for the Brognia Brothers produce company out in Henrietta and said that it was a good job. Eventually he got another job at G & G which he kept until his arrest. However, Shawcross maintained that he left Brognia Brothers because it was too difficult to maintain a commuting schedule from the city of Rochester to Henrietta. Other reports say that Brognia fired Shawcross when the owner learned about his prison record and his previous convictions.

Shawcross told Park Dietz that he was more than happy for the next few months working at G & G making salads and even helping them sell some of their products. He said that even after he had the fishing accident in which he fell eight feet down an embankment and had to spend twenty-one days on disability, he was able to go back to G & G with no problems. He said that he was still angry about having had to move from town to town, but he was trying to start life all over again. An important part about making another start, he said, was the need to integrate Rose—whom he wanted to marry—into his family. To do that, he said, he needed for his family to meet her. And that's where the ultimate trouble began.

"Near Christmastime of '87 I tried to get my family to come down to meet Rose. And I haven't seen them in so long. And they refused. Now that was just pressure. Built-up pressure. And it must have been building up because I didn't realize that I had a habit of just pushing things on the side and forget about it. Something bad happens. I just push it away. Then I got involved with a woman who lives on Clinton Street and she pressured me. She says she wants me to live there. I said, 'No. I'm living with Rose.' I told her, 'I'm on parole. I got to do what my parole officers say. They told me I got to live here. This is where I'm going to stay.' A couple of times I was riding home from work on my bike and she forced me off the road with her car coming down that hill by Mount Hope by the cemetery. She forced me off the road and I went right over a hedge and messed up the

283

bike. When that happened, I was a little concerned about Rose."

Shawcross continued. "I broke it off finally," he said. "About six, eight months, then she started coming around again. I tried to tell Rose I want to be a Mormon. She says, 'They don't do that no more.' I says, 'Sure they do.' The woman who was coming after me was . . . Clara Neal."

Then, in January, Art found out from his sister Jeannie, who lived in Greece, New York, that his mother and father, who had not answered his messages to visit him over Christmas, had in fact visited her. And with Rose in the other room complaining about her patients, and what they were doing to her, and listening to his sister Jeannie describe how Bessie Shawcross had not liked the clock he had bought her from out of the catalog, Shawcross could feel the hot sweat coming up through his shirt and out the top of his head. Before he realized it he was wringing wet, dripping with perspiration. Jeannie's voice was growing fainter on the phone. The lights around him were getting brighter and brighter and he didn't know why. Then he felt the need to be alone, to run, to go into the streets as he used to go into the woods when he was younger. But it was the sweating. It was the sweating that wouldn't stop that he was most afraid of.

Art walked out barely mumbling something to Rose. Rose knew he was angry. Art was still sweating, he had to get into the streets. Rose looked out the door, saw him pumping away on his bike, pedaling along the icy roads, disappearing deeper into the darkness of the February night.

Epilogue
The Search for
Arthur Shawcross

Arthur J. Shawcross confessed to the murders of ten women, most of whom were prostitutes, in Monroe County. At his trial, the defense argued that he was insane at the time he committed the murders and put up a spirited and dramatically riveting "multiple personality" defense. "He was not insane," jury foreman Robert Edwards said as he announced the verdicts in the ten counts of murder. "And he did not suffer extreme emotional disturbance." Shawcross was convicted of ten counts of murder in the second degree and sentenced to ten consecutive 25-year sentences in Monroe County and one in Wayne County. It is unlikely that he will ever get out of prison alive.

The Shawcross trial was one of the highest-rated television shows in Rochester in November, 1990. As the jurors and television audiences heard the testimony of how Arthur Shawcross strangled his victims, mutilated some of them, and ate the sex organs out of two of them, they reacted with horror and a morbid curiosity. The spectators were

also fascinated by the videotapes of Arthur Shawcross under hypnosis supervised by Dr. Dorothy
Lewis speaking in the voice of his mother, who, he
claimed, sodomized him with a broom handle and
in the voice of "Ariemes," a thirteenth-century cannibal who claimed he had a lust for blood. It was
a frightening testimony, but the jurors told newspapers afterward that they didn't believe he was really insane. Like the Steinberg trial, which captured
the imagination of New York City in 1988, the
Shawcross trial dominated the city of Rochester.
However, lost amid the publicity of the trial and
the charges and countercharges was the real Arthur
Shawcross. He was the person I was hired to explain.

Depending upon whom one chooses to believe,
Arthur Shawcross was either a fully manifested
"multiple," a flesh-eating cannibal, or a kindly
middle-aged man whose life was destroyed by Vietnam. I discovered a very different Arthur Shawcross, however, as I researched what others had
written about him and reviewed the medical tests
conducted on him. Arthur Shawcross was a mystery because of his seemingly passive and reticent
demeanor and his explosive temper and violent personality. What made him explode into rage? Why
did he kill Karen Ann Hill, Jack Blake, Dorothy
Blackburn, Dorothy Keller, June Stotts, Felicia
Stephens, Anna Marie Steffen, and the other
women?

I believe that Shawcross is one of the most vivid examples of what behavior severe post-traumatic stress, in combination with other biochemical, neurological, psychological, and social factors, can produce. Here is the evidence that I reviewed.

In March 1990, just two months after Shawcross's arrest and his confessions to state police investigators and Rochester city police detectives, Rochester clinical psychologist James Clark administered a battery of tests for the purposes of a psychological assessment. Dr. Clark seemed to believe Shawcross's stories of child abuse, sex abuse, and incest. He also seems to take seriously Shawcross's claims of atrocities he witnessed and participated in in Vietnam. Dr. Clark writes of Shawcross's description of his tour of duty in Vietnam "from his discussion, it appeared that his experiences in Vietnam were critical ones for him, and apparently established a course of much of his later life."

Dr. Clark said that Shawcross combined I.Q. of 95 placed him in the "average" range of intellect "at the 37th percentile." He reported further that "the difference between his verbal and performance I.Q.s is significant, and is in a range frequently associated with either learning disabilities, acting out behaviors, or both." In his other tests where he experienced frustration, Shawcross displayed severe temper reactions and seemed on the edge of physical violence. He often became reduced to physical activity and gesturing. "The rapid development of this sequence of behaviors when faced with frustration," Dr. Clark wrote, "perhaps offers a model for his behavior in other frustrating and angry circumstances." Dr. Clark also suggested evidence of a learning disability, anti-social behaviors, low self-image, low self-esteem, and organic impairment as a result of Shawcross's many head injuries.

In assessing Shawcross's personality, Dr. Clark pointed to the possibility of "denial as a defense mechanism along with limited personal insight." He suggested the possibility of a "disturbed and anxious man who recognizes his present situation would benefit from his 'looking sick.' Deteriorated defenses are indicated in the context of possible efforts to exaggerate his psychological difficulties. He also wrote that "the indirect expression of anger and hostility is also indicated." And that Shawcross might suffer from a moderate form of clinical depression for which medication might be prescribed. Dr. Clark also found that people like Shawcross could tend to "act-out sexually and/or aggressively with a truly amazing failure to look at what they are doing. Episodic acting-out of impulses may occur followed by periods of inhibition and restraint."

In addition, Dr. Clark said that Shawcross's performance on the psychopathic deviate scale meant that he might be "rebellious, non-conforming, and have a history of major conflict with society. Individuals in this range are characteristically dissatisfied with their family, their social lives, and people

290

in general. While they may relate well to others on a superficial level, they do not easily form close personal ties. Individuals of this sort are generally described as unreliable, with shallow feelings and loyalties, with frequent moodiness and resentment. Poor family and social ties are part of the picture along with acting-out of the 'I want, I want' variety. In the long run such people are shallow and superficial. They are not necessarily hostile toward other people, but they don't particularly care much for them either, except to the extent that they may be used to further their own ends and needs."

The report states further that "Mr. Shawcross's score on the paranoia scale and the schizophrenia scale clearly demonstrate his alienation from the mainstream, and his prickly sensitivity. Individuals scoring in these ranges actively blame others for their difficulties and frequently use the mechanism of projection."

In his summary, Dr. Clark said that Shawcross "harbors strong resentment against his mother and tends to see women in one of two different roles. Some are 'good women,' as much as his present wife. His bitter experiences with prostitutes in Vietnam have contributed to his second categorization of women as objects of mistrust and carriers of disease who are available for his personal pleasure." Finally, Dr. Clark noted that in the event Shawcross was convicted and sent to prison, "there is a possibility of suicidal ideation."

Shawcross, like most serial killers who hit the brick wall at the end of their killing careers, might be inclined to take his own life because there simply is nothing left to kill.

In September 1990, Professor Dorothy Otnow Lewis of the Department of Psychiatry of the NYU Medical Center evaluated Shawcross concurrent with her research as a defense expert in the Monroe County trial. Her report paid particular attention to Shawcross's head injuries as a child and young adult, his paralysis at the age of nine, his blackouts and episodes of falling, and episodes as an adult in which his second wife, Linda Neary, reported that he seemed to wander off and did not know where he had been. Dr. Lewis cites these and other episodes in which she cites Neary as saying that Shawcross seemed to "space out" and become unresponsive.

Regarding the paralysis that Shawcross himself talked about in his interviews and which his mother, Bessie, reported, Dr. Lewis suggested that it might be more accurate to categorize it as an hysterical paralysis. In evaluating Shawcross's psychiatric history, Dr. Lewis describes records that indicate that "as early as six years of age Mr. Shawcross was an extremely disturbed child, unable to function appropriately at home or at school. He could not sit still in class, made peculiar noises, hid under his desk, and had extreme difficulty making any friends at all. For these reasons he and his family were referred for counseling, but his father refused to participate and the interviewing never really got started. Records report that by age seven years he had tried to run away from home on more than one occasion, a phenomenon his mother dismissed as 'just hiding.' Although the threat to run away is characteristic of many children, the act of repeated attempts actually to flee home is strongly suggestive of severe physical and/or sexual abuse. As he got older, his behaviors appeared more and more peculiar. For example, according to his relatives, he would walk around, talking to himself and, from time to time, was overheard talking baby talk. This is noteworthy because he was overheard speaking this way as an adult. In spite of his being of normal intelligence, he kept failing his course and, at 18–19 years of age, still found himself in the ninth grade. He finally dropped out of school altogether."

Dr. Lewis cites Shawcross's inclination toward oral sex and his stated frequent attempts at oral sex with his female siblings. She says that his frequent masturbation and especially "the predilection for oral sexual activity are characteristic of youngsters who have been sexually abused by adults and taught behaviors not usually part of the repertoire of normal children."

Shawcross actively denied any sexual abuse on the part of his mother, Dr. Lewis reported. However, when, under hypnosis, "he was regressed to childhood, strong memories emerged of his mother's sexual behaviors toward him. He relived episodes in which his mother forced him to 'show me what Tina did,' and stimulate her orally. Then she brutally punished him."

Further in her report, Dr. Lewis wrote that Shawcross consciously remembered an incident of anal penetration by his mother when she gave him an enema and occasionally when she took his temperature rectally. However, under hypnosis, "he recalled vividly and painfully having large objects, including the stick of a broom, shoved deep into his rectum as punishment for his sexual activity with is sister and with Tina. One particular episode emerged in which he was severely injured, bled from his rectum, was doubled over, and could not move. This event, completely lost to conscious memory, is of special relevance because it is consistent with the records of his hospitalization for paralysis of his legs. It is also consistent with his mother's description of a time he was doubled over, couldn't move, and had to be hospitalized."

There is evidence, Dr. Lewis reported, that Arthur Shawcross was "severely" sexually abused and that early on "he developed a dissociative style of coping with his intolerable situation. Unable to express his rage at home, it spilled over into relationships with peers, and his episodic rages made him unpopular with other children. From childhood on, Mr. Shawcross was a loner, spending hours by himself in the woods." Shawcross had imaginary friends whom he spoke to and reported that his mother would speak to him "about his behaviors and his choice of women." He said that he tried to tell his mother that he regarded his sister Jeannie more like a wife than a sister and, he told Dr. Lewis and Dr. Dietz as well, it was the death of one of his sisters' boyfriends in Vietnam that prompted his request that he be sent to Vietnam instead of to Germany.

Dr. Lewis also lends some credence to Shawcross's Vietnam experiences even though she says that they are impossible to verify. She writes that "similar events have been reported by others returning from that war."

"It would seem that while in Vietnam, most likely as a result of the carnage witnessed," Dr. Lewis reported, "Mr. Shawcross decompensated to a point at which he was capable of extremely grotesque bizarre acts. He would wander through the woods, sensing a presence near him similar to the imaginary companions of his childhood. Mr. Shawcross described a particularly grotesque episode when he tortured and murdered two women, roasting and eating the flesh of one, and decapitating both. Whether or not this actually occurred or is a vivid fantasy has not been determined. The similarity, however, to Mr. Shawcross's subsequent behaviors with the women he murdered lends credence to his account. It would seem that Mr. Shawcross's experiences in Vietnam, whatever they were, further contributed to his mental instability. While still in the service, he was seen by a psychiatrist and according to his young wife [Linda Neary] she was told that she would have to sign a commitment paper in order to hospitalize him. This she did not feel comfortable doing and so he did not get treatment."

Dr. Lewis also describes the hypnotic therapy sessions during which Shawcross relived the abuse he claimed his mother inflicted upon him and at one point actually "seemed to flip into another character, that of his mother, and thus took on the role of the aggressor. This kind of phenomenon is characteristic of severely abused children who eventually dissociate to the point of becoming multiple personalities." In other interviews in which Shawcross was regressed under hypnosis to the episodes of the homicides, he said that his mother's voice was in his head, berating the woman he was with. In one session, his mother took over the interview, Dr. Lewis reported, and "she described holding the victim with one hand while Mr. Shawcross strangled her with the other."

Dr. Lewis summarized her report by saying that Shawcross was a "seriously psychiatrically impaired man who, as a result of early brutal abuse and subsequent war experiences, suffers from post-traumatic stress disorder, manifested primarily by dissociative episodes and extreme violence."

296

In my own preliminary report on this case, in which I solicited the advice and expertise of Dr. Vernon Mark for the defense team in Wayne County, I wrote that "I interviewed Mr. Shawcross on five separate occasions for a total of at least 24 hours. I also interviewed former wife, Linda Neary, his current wife, Rose Walley Shawcross, and his mistress, Clara Neal." I outlined the chronology of Shawcross's criminal activities, including his conviction on burglary of a Sears-Roebuck store in which he was placed on probation in the Youthful Offender Program, a subsequent burglary in which he received six months' probation, his claims of atrocities in Vietnam, his 1968 arson charges, and complaints of wife-beating lodged against him by wife Penny Sherbino, three petty larcenies in 1969, and the 1969 arson charges at Knowltons' and Crowley's, for which he was sent to Attica and then to Auburn. I also cited his murders of Jack Blake and Karen Ann Hill, his fifteen-year term at Green Haven, and the murders of the eleven women in Monroe and Wayne Counties for which he was about to stand trial.

I cited the following "signs, symptoms, and predisposing factors" for Dr. Mark:

1. Shawcross seemed older than his 44 years, he was 60 pounds overweight, and he had severe scars and scratches on his arms. He had severe psoriasis on his head and face, and every morning he awoke with fresh scratches on his arms that he said were

caused by his gouging himself in his sleep. I suggested that Shawcross might be engaging in self-mutilation or might have a severe biological or allergic reaction. Shawcross showed little emotion when confessing his crimes or telling his story, but he shows genuine sadness when asked about his biological family, primarily his mother.

2. Shawcross is cooperative and seemingly tireless in his efforts to tell his story. In fact, he becomes agitated and sometimes angry when an interviewer makes an error reflecting a segment of his sometimes tedious verbalization for clarification. He is almost hypermnesic in his vivid recall of the details of events leading up to the act of violence. He also writes letters, but he is overly verbal and has little humor.

3. From biochemical and biogenetic testing we discovered two predisposing genetic and psychogenic factors: the 47-XYY chromosonal keriotype, and pyluria diagnosed because of a 200 reading of kryptopyrolles. The average is 5, and 10 is high. These conditions, experts say, in the very least produce a weakened ability to deal with stress. He was given the test twice, once when he was under a lot of stress and the number was 200. A retest was given when he was under moderate stress and the reading was 75. These are way above average, and the 200 count was actually off the scale.

4. He has a history of at least four documented head traumas which required hospitalization. In

1962 he was hit on top of the head with a stone. In May 1962 he was hit in the forehead with a discus, was knocked unconscious, and was required to stay in the hospital for three days. In August 1963, he was hit in the head with a sledgehammer and knocked unconscious. When he was in the service he fell from a ladder while trying to put up a tent, was knocked unconscious, and had to go to the hospital. In addition to these documented injuries, Shawcross was also active in football and wrestling in high school and was constantly jostled and placed at risk for head and neck injuries that did not require hospitalization. He was knocked out at the gate of Attica when he was an inmate there and was accident-prone throughout his life. Shawcross complains of headaches when under stress and complained of headaches during his tour of duty in Vietnam.

5. Shawcross required little sleep during his freedom from prison. He only slept three to four hours a day.

6. During the episodes of violence, Shawcross has described the following physiological changes after he had been threatened and becomes enraged: "Lights get ten times brighter," and "I hear little or no sound . . . sometimes I hear a woman's voice behind me but look around and no one is there."

Shawcross also reports beginning to sweat profusely, especially on his face, head, and upper torso. He reports smelling a strong urine smell "like a farmyard or barnyard."

"At that moment, I don't realize anything around me. I lose all sense of feeling. I lose all sense of time . . . I forget everything."

"Throughout my life, when something bad happens to me, I push it to the side and later it comes out."

During the episodes he claims a tingling around his mouth, chin, lips, hands, arms, and feet.

He claims that the first time he had such a set of symptoms was in Vietnam, after seeing a young Vietnamese boy blown apart.

Throughout his life, Shawcross claims to have repressed his memories but once he begins talking, he remembers vivid detail. It should also be noted that he has gone over the stories many times with police, psychiatrists, and his attorneys. There remain gaps in his memory.

He says that the episodes last about four hours and that the sweating lasts about 25 minutes. The episodes seemed to become more severe and longer lasting as time went by. He also seemed to have more trouble repressing the memory of the events.

During the violent episodes . . . "I get bigger . . . other times in my life I have had the feeling of leaving my body."

His wives and girlfriends report that he has spells when he stares off into space and they have to call his name or shake him to get a response.

He also claims to have had episodes of walking

or driving and ending up somewhere and not knowing where he was or how he got there. His two wives interviewed for this report corroborate these experiences.

7. During the time he was a free man, Shawcross describes a compulsive tendency to always be on the move. During the time of release, he was married, had at least two other romantic affairs, became the father figure to one of his girlfriend's families, participated in a drug-selling business, took care of some homeless people, "dated" about a hundred prostitutes, and fished and hunted deer. All the while he was on the go — taking long walks, riding his bicycle, and when he could, borrowing a car from girlfriend Clara Neal for long drives on which he picked up prostitutes.

Throughout his life, he has taken long walks alone, or long bicycle rides when he would become upset about something. This compulsive, perhaps hyperactive behavior, has been corroborated by others.

8. Arthur Shawcross claims a history of incest with his Aunt Tina, his sister Jeannie, and his cousin Linda. He claims verbal and physical abuse by his mother and emotional abandonment by his father at age nine.

His mother and sister firmly deny the sexual and physical abusive situations.

While these claims cannot be independently documented, the disenfranchisement from his family is well-documented. His family has not seen him in twenty-plus years, and even though they agreed to see prosecuting investigators and psychiatrists, they refused to see those of us working for the defense.

Throughout his records are claims by him of love/hate feelings toward his mother.

He has described his father as a completely passive man who, he says, is completely controlled by his mother.

Rose Walley Shawcross, Linda Neary, and Clara Neal all admitted to being mother figures to Arthur. They all profess love for him and when asked why, refer to his neediness. They all, including Shawcross himself, strongly react when speaking about the mother. They all become teary when speaking about the rejections Arthur says he has felt from his mother.

It appears from interviews that the last rejection by the mother was one of the precipitating factors of the spree of murders in Monroe and Wayne Counties. Shawcross claims that he had not gone out with prostitutes before February 1989. During the Christmas 1988 holidays Arthur and Rose bought a $49 clock with a picture of Jesus for Arthur's mother. They sent it to her by mail. The gift was rejected. Bessie Shawcross reportedly told her daughter Jeannie that "I don't want that kind of religion in my house." The Shawcross parents also reportedly rejected repeated invitations to drive down the fifty miles from Watertown to see their

302

son after his parole from Green Haven. They had not seen him in about twenty years. He could not go to Watertown to see his parents because of the child murders. The mother had anger for Rose and Arthur during the 1987 Christmas season, yet during the same period she went to visit his sister. After the rejection of the gift, Shawcross had a severe bout with depression and headaches. It was just over one month later that he went out with the first prostitute, Dorothy Blackburn, and murdered her.

Arthur is the eldest of the four Shawcross siblings. His mother was pregnant with him before she was married. He was an unplanned and unwanted child. He has always felt that he was a "doorstep" baby. He felt that he looked different from the rest of the family.

9. Incest, sexual abuse, bestiality, necrophilia, pedophilia, rape, murder, cannibalism, hyposexuality, and homosexuality have all been claimed by Shawcross.

Hyposexuality is well documented independently. "I only had one orgasm since 1987 and that was with my wife, Rose." This occurred when they'd just met, before they were married. He went out with prostitutes to find out what was wrong with him. He kept trying to have an ejaculation, but to no avail. Linda Neary said that after Vietnam he had sexual problems and the only way she could get him in "a good mood" would be to hold him like a child during foreplay.

The mother and sister deny abuse and incest, but this does not prove it did not happen. Dr. Lewis believes the incest story.

Cannibalism, rape, and murder are also well-documented in the convictions out of Watertown and the current charges that have been filed against him in Rochester.

10. Several events in his life would possibly qualify Shawcross for Post-Traumatic Stress Disorder:

A. Sexual abuse by his aunt and possibly his mother.

B. Chronic rejection by his family.

C. A friend's father's death, of a heart attack, in a room alone with Arthur when he was eight.

D. Shawcross's claims of having been raped when he was fourteen and of being forced to give oral sex to the brother of a young girl he was having sexual relations with.

E. Vietnam, where he claims he saw hundreds of people killed and where he himself murdered a child, raped and cannibalized women, and murdered peasants. He states that his symptoms began in Vietnam.

F. Being a child killer in Attica made him a "short eyes," a "low man" at the bottom of the prison hierarchy. He was threatened repeatedly with death and with being "piped" or beaten with metal pipes. He claims he was raped and had to defend himself against other prisoners. He was living in a constant state of stress. He was forced to eat on the floor and not at the table with the other prisoners.

G. He was in the prison riot at Attica and saved a guard's life.

H. Shawcross was literally chased from three upstate New York communities when people in these towns discovered that he was a convicted child killer. This is well documented by parole reports as well as by Shawcross's own recollections.

I. Final rejection by his mother and family causing a kind of "atypical" grief.

11. Shawcross claimed his cannibalism began in Vietnam but was precipitated when he was a butcher at age eighteen. He claimed to have begun eating raw meat at that time and drinking animals' blood daily for about a year when he was learning to dismember them. Cannibalism and a fixation on raw flesh is one of the side effects of severe pyrroluria disorders. About thirty percent of all serial killers in my initial survey were cannibals. Interestingly, the form of pyrroluria that Shawcross has lists cannibalism as one of its symptoms, especially when combined with B-complex vitamin deficiencies.

12. Although Shawcross claimed that he had no problems with alcohol, he went on to explain that as a young man he would become "drunk" by imbibing just one beer or even being around the fumes of alcohol. This sounds like "idiosyncratic

intoxication," which is one of the symptoms of temporal lobe epilepsy. Shawcross became better with age, and his wife, Linda Neary, reported that once, prior to killing her dog in a fit of rage and beating her, causing a miscarriage, Shawcross drank excessively.

Corroborating much of what I said in my report, Dr. Richard Kraus, a Rochester psychiatrist, stated that Shawcross did have elevated levels of kryptopyrroles which "identify individuals at high risk for becoming violent." These clinical correlates of these abnormally high levels of kryptopyrroles in humans are "partial disorientation, abnormal EEGs, general nervousness, depression, episodes of dizziness, chest and abdominal pains, progressive loss of ambition, poor social performance, and decreased sexual potency, all of which are found in the history of Arthur Shawcross." In addition, other behavioral correlates are "marked irritability, rages, terrible problems with stress control, diminished ability to control stress, inability to control anger once provoked, mood swings, poor memory, a preference for nighttime, violence, and antisocial behavior."

Dr. Kraus's findings were also interesting in that they correlated Shawcross's levels of kryptopyrolles with his brainwave activity indicating a degree of brain damage and neurologic impairment. He said that "the psychological test finding of 'modest organicity' is supported by these findings. Mr. Shawcross does have a neurologic impairment in his ability to reason and to exercise sound judgment." Moreover, his computerized EEG showed patterns of dysfunction similar to patients who experience seizures, especially those who might be diagnosed as having temporal lobe epilepsy. The computerized EEG could contribute to an explanation of Shawcross's violent behavior, to his blackouts (in conjunction with his abnormally high levels of kryptopyrolles), and to his feelings of "aura" preceding his violent episodes.

In other words, I discovered, Shawcross had a medical condition in addition to his psychological and antisocial behavior disorders and Post-Traumatic Stress Disorder. All of this was potentiated by his inability to deal with authority. This condition was evidenced as early as elementary school as a learning disorder which could have been correlated with his XYY genetic disorder. XYY male children are often loners or runaways and act differently from everyone else. They are prone to rage and to getting into violent interactions with others. Given this genetic condition in conjunction with his other conditions, it was probably impossible for him to mediate his behavior in any way.

The real Arthur Shawcross probably had very little chance for success without dramatic intervention in his life at a very early age. Like Henry Lee Lucas and other serial killers, Shawcross displays a typical pattern of aberrant behavior that can be red-flagged at an early age and traced through his life. Even his wild claims of violent behavior and his self-importance at critical moments of violence — hypergrandiosity — are typical of serial killers in their fantasies. We probably shouldn't indulge in pointing accusing fingers at the people in Shawcross's life who didn't intervene. It's too late for that. Rather, we should worry about the next generation of Arthur Shawcross types moving through the elementary grades of our inner-city school systems.